THE SCHOOL OF THE SPIRIT

An Introduction to Spirit-Filled Ministry

Will & Jaime Riddle

3rd Edition

Published by: Kingdom Change.

Please contact the author at will@kingdomchange.org if you would like to reproduce this book or sections of the book for your own purposes. All personal correspondence will receive a reply.

Printed in the United States of America
ISBN 978-0-9997895-3-7

Table of Contents

HOW TO USE THIS BOOK

Goals of the School

The School of the Spirit was written to build a healthy culture of Holy Spirit based ministry in a church setting, and to help indviduals have a comprehensive understanding of Holy Spirit basics. The *School of the Spirit* is a resource that pastors can trust. Many pastors are eager for a greater expression of the Holy Spirit but concerned about the impact it might have on their ability to reach lost people or to manage expectations of the congregation. *The School* was developed in the context of a mainstream non-denominational church and is intended to be accessible to regular people.

So many times, in church settings we find either disuse of the spiritual gifts or misuse of the spiritual gifts, or we find emphasis of one gift at the expense of the others. Our goal is to build a culture of passionate pursuit while providing healthy guidelines. If our church can do it, *so can yours.* We have seen great answers to prayer without the many of the complications sometimes associated with Spirit-filled ministry.

We have seen great fruit using this manual in different contexts. For some, it has provided a safe introduction to the Holy Spirit in a loving environment. For others, burned by misuse of spiritual gifts, it has provided an on-ramp back into eager pursuit of the fulness of what He can do. For those who have been in unrestrained environments, it has provided a healthy context to express their gifting.

We encourage you to include and invite couples to do it together because exaggerate when we say that we have seen marriages healed and callings restored just by taking people on this journey. Often, we meet people who say "my spouse likes to pray, but not me" and yet as they walk the journey together, God tunes them for use together in ministry.

Group Format

The School of the Spirit is designed for use as a 12-week small group curriculum and to be led by a mature Spirit-filled believer or ideally a couple. We intentionally try to recruit a full class each semester of people with the best capacity to be on a ministry. Those with life experience, stability, and a Spirit-filled background of some kind are the ideal participants, but the School will work for people from many starting points. Remember that the gifts of the Holy Spirit are power tools. Using power tools requires training so that people do not get hurt, and to use them in a public setting, that requires maturity and trust.

Each chapter of the book has a Scripture driven teaching covering several major topics. During the **first hour** the leaders should teach the material for that session. We want everything we do to be rooted and grounded in the example and teaching of Scripture, and we want the community to be built around a shared understanding of what that is.

At the end of the teaching in each chapter we provide questions to help foster an educational discussion. People learn best when they have the opportunity to consider how material interacts with their own lives and personal history. This helps make the teaching real and relevant. Therefore, we encourage you to try and allow time for the question time.

At the end of the chapter, we have then provided a relevant activation, where people get to practice together. During the **second hour** we break up into micro-groups (of 6 or less), each with a leader, and do the activation. These activations allow people to get to know each other better, and practice what they learned in a safe-environment., and these smaller groups create a safe space and ensure that everyone has sufficient time to interact and participate. During the activation we encourage you to provide light coaching to your potential team members. This not only helps people develop, it helps them get used to ministering under leadership, which is essential for all healthy ministry.

Finally, we include a section of "Steps You Can Take" so that people can develop and activate further on their own time. While most people will tend to walk away and forget, we want those who are hungry to have the ability to continue to practice, activate and grow.

RELATIONSHIP

RELATIONSHIP WITH JESUS

Ministry impact does not come from doctrines, it comes from relationship. Cultivation of a personal relationship with God is the most important part of seeing answered prayer.

> *God created man in his own image, in the image of God he created him; male and female he created them –Genesis 1:27*

God created us with a personality and with feelings, reflecting how He is. Yet, we rarely think of an understand God in these terms. The foundation of a good relationship with God is relating to Him like a person.

> *Whoever does not love does not know God, because **God is love**. –1 John 4:8*

After we realize that God is personal, we need to know what kind of person He is. He is not harsh or condemning, but rather, he is **love**. When we have harsh ideas about God it blocks our ability to commune with Him.

> *I am the vine; you are the branches. If you remain in me and I in you, you will bear much fruit; apart from me you can do nothing. –John 15:5*

Abiding means spending time with Jesus allowing him to shape and direct your heart and life.   Your private time alone with Jesus softening your heart toward him and listening to his voice are the keystone.

> *Seek the LORD while he may be found; call on him while he is near. –Isaiah 55:6*

> *Ask and it will be given to you; seek and you will find; knock and the door will be opened to you. For everyone who asks receives; the one who seeks finds; and to the one who knocks, the door will be opened. –Matthew 7:7-8*

We should not be frustrated when our initial efforts at drawing close to God do not yield as much as we had hoped.   The Bible encourages us to seek, because it takes time for us to postures ourselves to be close to Him, and to learn how to stay connected to Him.

> *If you love me, keep my commands. – John 14:15*

Many people are hindered in relationship simply because they are not obeying the general will of God. When you harbor negative thoughts toward others, or live any kind of compromised lifestyle, it blocks your ability to be close to God.

> *My son, pay attention to what I say; turn your ear to my words. Do not let them out of your sight, keep them within your heart; for they are life to those who find them and health to one's whole body. – Proverb 4:20-22*

God's words of love and affirmation over us are life and health to us. We are only able to stay close as we begin to live from these words.

Ministering His Presence

> And he said to him, "If your presence will not go with me, do not bring us up from here. —Exodus 33:15

God's presence is a real thing. Moses did not want to go to enter the Promised Land without God. We want to cultivate that lifestyle of His Presence. You can minister the presence to someone, and you can minister *from* the presence. If you minister to an unbeliever, it is not uncommon at all for them to tangibly feel God touching them.

> And he said, "My presence will go with you, and I will give you rest."
> —Exodus 33:14

> You make known to me the path of life; in your presence there is fullness of joy... —Psalm 16:11

We recognize His presence by what it brings. Joy, rest, and the other fruits of the Spirit (Gal 5:22-23) are all signs that we are encountering His presence. Even though Christ is always in us, we can see a greater or lesser manifestation of His presence in our lives and in our corporate services.

> "I am the vine; you are the branches. If you remain in me and I in you, you will bear much fruit; apart from me you can do nothing. — John 5:15

If we live in His presence and minister out of that, everyone who attends our services will eventually know that whatever their need, our church is a place where they can receive prayer, love, and ministry.

> "He must increase, but I must decrease. — John 3:30

John gives one of the keys to experience more of God's presence. Instead of being conscious of yourself, or of others, become conscious of Jesus working through and with you. Celebrate His greatness, He will do amazing things. Jesus is the one who does the ministry. Posture your heart in alignment with His.

> For in Christ Jesus, neither circumcision nor uncircumcision has any value. The only thing that counts is **faith expressing itself through love**.
> —Galatians 5:6

In ministry, the natural expression of faith should always be from a loving and selfless position in our hearts. When you are praying for someone, you are a conduit between God and that person. You need to be connected to God in faith, and to the person in love. When you pray for others posture yourself in the same place where you receive God's love, and allow Him to flow through you to them.

APPROACHING THE HOLY SPIRIT

Ministry doesn't just happen to individuals. Ministry happens in a culture. The goal of the School of the Spirit is to build a culture of pastoral and supernatural ministry in your group. We believe close relationship with God and with each other is the best paradigm for that ministry. We seek to grow together in our ability to change lives by the power of the Holy Spirit. Below are some of the key principles we follow:

We Eagerly Seek for God to do More

> *Pursue love, and earnestly desire the spiritual gifts, especially that you may prophesy. – 1 Corinthians 14:1*

Our church seeks the full expression of all the gifts of the Holy Spirit to operate within the Body.

> *Heal the sick, raise the dead, cleanse those who have leprosy, drive out demons. Freely you have received; freely give. – Matthew 10:8*

God is supernatural, and He wants us to be supernatural. He wants to change lives through us. We are cultivating a supernatural atmosphere together where prayers are answered, breakthrough are expected, and healings are normal. The Lord will touch His people.

> *Since you are so eager to have the special abilities the Spirit gives, **seek** those that will **strengthen the whole church**. – 1 Corinthians 14:12*

Paul tells us to pursue spiritual gifts because we want to build up the church. Seeing God work among us in notable ways requires intentional seeking. Sometimes this is called **consecration**, or setting yourself apart to be used by God in a special way. Our prayer team sets itself apart to pursue God in a special way.

We Pursue Love

> ***Pursue love,*** *and earnestly desire the spiritual gifts… – 1 Corinthians 14:1*

Love is the very most important thing. We cultivate a heart of love so that when people ask for prayer, they experience Jesus' love through us.

> *By this everyone will know that you are my disciples: if you love one another. – John 13:35*

We are rock solid in our belief that it is always God's desire for the good and redemptive thing. We never judge or condemn those we pray for. We use our faith in the context of blessing others and building them up, rather than correction.

Love is patient and kind; love does not envy or boast; it is not arrogant or rude. It does not insist on its own way; it is not irritable or resentful it does not rejoice at wrongdoing, but rejoices with the truth. Love bears all things, believes all things, hopes all things, endures all things.
−1 Corinthians 13:4-7

Paul gives us a model of what love looks like, which we develop over a lifetime. The very most important thing when you pray for someone is that they feel that you love them, and that God is loving them through you. It's about them, not about you.

We are Naturally Supernatural

If the whole church assembles together and all speak in tongues, and ungifted men or unbelievers enter, will they not say that you are mad? But if all prophesy, and an unbeliever or an ungifted man enters, he is convicted by all, he is called to account by all; the secrets of his heart are disclosed; and so he will fall on his face and worship God, declaring that God is certainly among you.
−1 Corinthians 14:23-25

Using spiritual gifts requires moving outside of what is rational, but we can present what God is doing in ways that are relatable to anyone. We want to be supernatural but as normal as possible: **naturally supernatural**. When we look closely at the life of Jesus, we see Him do many supernatural things which are so subtle, that they can almost be missed:

- He told Nathanael that He saw him under the fig tree before he was called. (John 1:48)
- He called Zacchaeus by name in the tree. (Luke 19:5)
- The woman with the issue of blood was healed by touching the hem of His garment. (Luke 6:19)

Jesus was at one with the Father (John 30:30) and therefore it was natural and normal for Him to be miraculous.

*If I speak in the tongues of men and of angels, but have not love, I am a noisy gong or a clanging cymbal. And if I have prophetic powers, and understand all mysteries and all knowledge, and if I have all faith, so as to remove mountains, but have not love, I am nothing. If I give away all I have, and if I deliver up my body to be burned, **but have not love, I gain nothing.*** *−1 Corinthians 13:1-3*

If we are amazingly supernatural, but the person isn't loved, we failed. We never allow our desire for spiritual power to overtake our love for others.

Most of the time, the work of God is discreet or unobtrusive, but sometimes God does something which produces a dramatic response. We should not be surprised when we pray if God touches someone, since that's what we're asking for! When we sense that God is working, it's important that we allow Him to work and collaborate with what He is doing. We would rather you take risks and let us guide you, than for you to not take risks and miss the moving of the Holy Spirit.

On the other hand, sometimes a person we pray for may be so eager to show that God is touching them, that they act in disruptive ways--uncontrolled shaking, spontaneously making loud noises, moving around dramatically, or falling over in response to prayer as a matter of expectation. As ministers, we don't draw attention to these things, but keep our eyes on what God is doing.

We Cultivate a Safe Atmosphere

> *The spirits of prophets are subject to the control of the prophets.*
> *– 1 Corinthians 14:32*

The Corinthian church that Paul was very eager for the Spiritual gifts, but in their eagerness for the Spirit to move, they failed to govern the operation of the Holy Spirit.

> *Let all things be done decently and in order. – 1 Corinthians 14:40*

The Bible teaches that we both can and should govern the operation of the Holy Spirit so that all are edified.

> *The one who speaks in a tongue builds up himself, but the one who prophesies builds up the church. – 1 Corinthians 14:4*

One of their problems was that they did not recognize the distinction between public and private worship. In a public meeting, it's important that we be aware of others, and act in such a way that edifies everyone, not draws attention to ourselves.

> *If a revelation comes to someone who is sitting down, the first speaker should stop. For you can all prophesy in turn so that everyone may be instructed and encouraged. –1 Corinthians 14:30-32*

It is also important to have guidelines and protocol that creates a safe, effective environment.

> *I thank God that I speak in tongues more than all of you. But in the church I would rather speak five intelligible words to instruct others than ten thousand words in a tongue. – 1 Corinthians 14:18-19*

We desire all of our prayer ministers to pray in tongues to build up their spirit, but while we are ministering, we are sensitive to a person's background and experience.

MINISTRY MODEL

Effective ministry is more than prayer. It begins with our greeting and continues through to the instructions we give as they leave. The ALMA model below will help you remember each part of effective ministry:

> ➤ **A**sk the person what they want prayer for.
> ➤ **L**isten carefully to what they say
> ➤ **M**inister to their need
> ➤ **A**ctivate the person to take the appropriate next step

Ask

> *When I called, you answered me; you greatly emboldened me.*
> *—Psalm 138:3*

When someone feels that God has heard them, they are changed and bonded to Him for life. The first step of prayer ministry is to *listen* to what the person wants to share. Ask, "How can I pray for you?" and listen carefully. Do your best to identify with exactly where the person is, and then come alongside with an ear of encouragement and support. Men especially may want to practice being pastoral, asking questions, and having the right facial expressions.

Listen

> *Now **you** are the body of Christ, and each one of you is a part of it.*
> *– 1 Corinthians 12:27*

When you pray for someone you are representing Jesus. You are His Body. People are responding to God, and you are there to represent Him.

> *Then you will call on me and come and pray to me, and **I will listen to you**. –*
> *Jeremiah 29:12*

One of God's most salient attributes is that He listens. We do not pray to a God who is deaf, but to one who hears.

> *I love the Lord, **for he heard my voice**;*
> *he heard my cry for mercy.*
> *Because he turned his ear to me,*
> *I will call on him as long as I live.*
> *– Psalm 116:1-2*

Listening is the gateway to someone's heart. Sometimes just listening releases healing, or faith to receive whatever God wants to minister. Don't feel you have to rush into praying before knowing what the Holy Spirit wants you to pray for.

Minister

"Ask, and it shall be given to you. Seek, and you shall find. Knock, and the door will be opened. Because everyone who asks, receives; he who seeks, finds; he who knocks, the door will be opened."
—Matthew 7:7-8

After we have listened to the person requesting prayer, we are ready to minister as the Holy Spirit leads. If we need to pray for healing, wisdom, an opportunity, or freedom, we believe God will move through us to provide it.

Activate

Activation is how a person follows through on what you have prayed together. When you are finished praying, look for an appropriate next step you can suggest for the person you're ministering to. Many people who come for prayer are looking for connection, healing, or helpful relationships. Apply natural insight and the leading of the Spirit. Here are some of the most obvious actions you can consider:

➤ **Serving:** Is there an opportunity for the person to develop relationships by joining a service activity through the church? Sometimes getting outside of ourselves can help us be more healthy

➤ **Small Groups.** What kind of small group or activity would bring them into community with others who can support and challenge them.

➤ **Freedom Ministry.** If you get the sense that they are working through deeper personal issues, they may need more extended ministry, either through a group or extended meeting with someone trained in this ministry.

➤ **More Prayer.** Invite the person to come back again if they want prayer for the same issue. Also, you can suggest the Wednesday night prayer meeting.

➤ **Potential Friend:** Who can you introduce them to that might help them on their journey or make them feel more at home at our Church? A person who can be a good friend or lead them to a potential set of friends? Feel free to connect them right there if possible, while many people can be found on Sunday.

➤ **Resources.** Is there a good book or sermon you can recommend for the person based on where they are?

The Ministry Moment

Communicate Love.   When someone wants ministry, do everything you know how to do to communicate love to them. This begins with a warm greeting and a smile. Then give them your undivided attention. Echo their struggles, show concern for their pain, touch them if it seems appropriate. Take cues from the person you are praying for about what they need to feel connected, and ask if you are not sure—"Is it ok if I...?"

Follow the Holy Spirit. Every situation is different and every person is different. As you ask, and listen, be sensitive to how the Lord would have you pray for them.

Gender Sensitivity. It is important to avoid situations where a man and woman are praying alone together because it can create emotional bonds that may lead to temptation on our end or theirs, or it could lead to the appearance that someone in appropriate is going on. If someone of the opposite sex seeks you out for prayer, don't shame them, just look for a discreet way to include someone of their same sex.

Major Issues. Prayer moments are powerful, but big situations often need times of extended prayer or ongoing support. Recognize the situation you are in, and give what you can at that time. If a person is open to deeper ministry and you have the time, it is great to provide extended ministry, while the Spirit is moving.

QUESTIONS:

1. How has your experience with spiritual gifts in the church shaped your feelings about seeking them and expressing them at church? What are your feelings about the naturally supernatural approach?
2. What are your experiences praying for people either individually, at an altar, or in a group? How do they compare with what we have presented here?
3. What are your experiences receiving prayer, at the altar or elsewhere? How have those experiences informed your views on prayer ministry?

ACTIVATION

Opener. Today we will practice greeting and praying for one another using the basic prayer model. Break into small groups of 2 or 3 and pray for each other using the model below: ALMA.

1. **A**sk what the problem is.
2. **L**isten to them share.
3. **M**inister the way the Holy Spirit leads you.
4. **A**ct. Identify an action that the person can take as a next step.

Try not to go too long on each step. Avoid counseling sessions. Minister from a position of love and listening to the Holy Spirit.

STEPS YOU CAN TAKE:

1. Consider one or two practical things you can do to take another step in your level of consecration so that you can operate in more love and power.
2. Practice the ALMA model of prayer on someone this week. Record any testimonies or questions you have after this experience, to bring to the next meeting.
3. Study the small groups on the our church website and become familiar with what resources are available for those we minister to.

4.

FAITH

LIVING BY FAITH

We all have faith, but it is good to review the basics of faith and build a strong foundation for God to move through. This helps us as prayer leaders and those we pray for.

Your Belief About God

> *But without faith it is impossible to please Him. For he that comes to God must believe **that He is**, and **that He is a rewarder** of those who diligently seek Him.*
> *—Hebrews 11:6*

In order to move in faith, we need two fundamental beliefs. First, that God is, meaning that He is the greatest reality in the universe and therefore able to do everything we might ask. Second, that he rewards those who seek him, meaning that he is good.

> *"Ask, and it shall be given to you. Seek, and you shall find. Knock, and the door will be opened. Because everyone who asks, receives; he who seeks, finds; he who knocks, the door will be opened."*
> *—Matthew 7:7-8*

Because God is good, our seeking will result in what we are seeking. To move in faith we must strengthen ourselves in this belief.

> *The thief comes only to steal, kill, and destroy. But I have come so that they might have life, and have it to the full. —John 10:10*

It can be hard to believe God is always for us, and that he desires to give us what we ask for. This is because the devil likes to switch his character for God's. But God is always good and the devil is always evil.

> *Every good and perfect gift is from above, coming down from the Father of the heavenly lights, who does not change like shifting shadows.*
> *—James 1:17*

> *And this is the message we heard and announce to you all: that God is light and in Him there is no darkness at all. —1 John 1:5*

When you feel like you can't get out of your situation, or that what you're struggling with is impossible, that is not God but the devil. God always wants you out, and he wants those you love out too. This gives you the faith to pursue the victory you're looking for.

Living as Though Dead

> *I have been crucified with Christ. It is no longer I who live, but Christ who lives in me. And the life I now live in the flesh, I live by faith in the Son of God, who loved me and gave himself for me. –Galatians 2:20*

After trusting God's goodness, the foundation of faith is to live as though dead.   If you are alive to your own desires, you cannot move in faith because you will be prevented by fear of losing what you desire. Moving in faith requires the willingness to risk your reputation and your life.

> *Nebuchadnezzar answered and said to them, "Is it true, O Shadrach, Meshach, and Abednego, that you do not serve my gods or worship the golden image that I have set up? … If you do not worship, you shall immediately be cast into a burning fiery furnace. And who is the god who will deliver you out of my hands?" Shadrach, Meshach, and Abednego answered and said to the king, "O Nebuchadnezzar, we have no need to answer you in this matter. If this be so, our God whom we serve is able to deliver us from the burning fiery furnace, and he will deliver us out of your hand, O king.* **But if not, be it known to you, O king, that we will not serve your gods** *or worship the golden image that you have set up." –Daniel 3:14-18*

Shadrach, Meshach, and Abednego believed and declared that God would deliver them from the furnace. But more importantly, they were willing to stake their lives on it.   The devil in this situation was intimidating, but God showed who really deserved the hell they were being threatened with. The end result was not only that the righteous were delivered, but they were promoted!   The reward we want is always on the other side of risk.

> *As Jesus was walking beside the Sea of Galilee, he saw two brothers, Simon called Peter and his brother Andrew…"Come follow me," Jesus said, "and I will make you fishers of men." Immediately, they left their nets and followed him. – Matthew 4:18-20*

When Peter and Andrew threw down their nets, they showed their faith through their willingness to risk it all—even their livelihood.

> *From that time Jesus began to show his disciples that he must go to Jerusalem and suffer many things from the elders and chief priests and scribes, and be killed, and on the third day be raised. And Peter took him aside and began to*

rebuke him, saying, "Far be it from you, Lord! This shall never happen to you." But he turned and said to Peter, "Get behind me, Satan! You are a hindrance to me. For you are not setting your mind on the things of God, but on the things of man." —Matthew 16:21-23

Jesus knew that faith would require Him to die. Peter did not yet understand the principle of living as though dead. You cannot look with your natural eyes and make natural plans if you want to live by faith.

Seeing with the Eyes of Faith

Faith comes by hearing, and hearing by the Word of Christ.
—Romans 10:17

You can live by what you see in the natural, but God wants you to live by what he is speaking to you.

They gave Moses this account: "We went into the land to which you sent us, and it does flow with milk and honey! Here is its fruit. But the people who live there are powerful, and the cities are fortified and very large..." Then Caleb silenced the people before Moses and said, "We should go up and take possession of the land, for we can certainly do it." But the men who had gone up with him said, "We can't attack those people; they are stronger than we are." —Numbers 13:27-31

Moses sent twelve spies into the Promised Land. Ten of the spies saw the size of the problem, but Caleb believed God was bigger than the opposition. Even though it was great, he knew God was much greater because he was in faith. He did not rely on what his natural eyes saw.

[Abraham] is our father in the sight of God, in whom he believed, even God, who gives life to the dead and calls the things that are not, as though they were. Against all hope, Abraham in hope believed and so became the father of many nations just as it had been said to him, "So should your offspring be." Without weakening in his faith, though his body was as good as dead—since he was about a hundred years old and Sarah's womb was also dead—yet he did not waver through unbelief regarding the promise of God but was strengthened in his faith and gave glory to God, fully persuaded that God had power to do what he had promised. – Romans 4:16-21

Abraham's faith began by obeying God to leave everything he knew, but it culminated in having a child at 100 years old and being willing to put that child on the altar. He was able to see beyond the natural. He did see reality, but also saw God's greater reality.

Living in faith is not about magic or denying what is in front of you, but in believing that God's greater reality always overrides the reality you're in.

CULTIVATING YOUR FAITH

It is not enough to know what faith is, we must cultivate it in order to see victories for the Lord.

Your Partnership with God

All authority in heaven and on earth has been given to me. Therefore go and make disciples of all nations, baptizing them in the name of the Father and of the Son and of the Holy Spirit, and teaching them to obey everything I have commanded you. And surely I am with you always, to the very end of the age. –Matthew 28:18-20

Jesus commanded the disciples to go and do God's will. He did not tell them to wait for a leading or to depend on a leading. They had heard the general will of God, so they went.

For all who are led by the Spirit of God are sons of God. – Romans 8:14

At the same time, specific leading is important. Living by faith is not unilateral. It depends both on you obeying the general will of God on your own, as well as you seeking the specific leading of the Holy Spirit.

"Come over to Macedonia and help us." –Acts 16:9

The life of faith is a partnership between you and God. You step out and do what you believe is right, but then you also look for God's leading and direction. This is what happened to Paul when the Spirit told him to go to Macedonia. He was out doing the general will of God when he received a more specific leading.

The Seed of Faith

The kingdom of heaven is like a mustard seed, which a man took and planted in his field. Though it is the smallest of all seeds, yet when it grows, it is the largest of garden plants and becomes a tree, so that the birds come and perch in its branches." –Matthew 13:32

The seed of the Kingdom is in your heart. Even though it is in seed form, you can cultivate it to become the largest tree in the garden so that others are able to rest in the branches of your faith.

"Truly I tell you, if you have faith as small as a mustard seed, you can say to this mountain, 'Move from here to there,' and it will move. Nothing will be impossible for you." –Matthew 17:20

Our natural minds struggle with this verse, but faith is not an intellectual thing. Faith is often informed by the mind, but is actually a trust and reliance in the heart. Even in seed form, faith is able to move mountains. As you cultivate that seed, you are able to do the impossible.

> *Now to him who is able to do exceedingly abundantly above all we could ever ask or think, according to the power that works within us...*
> *–Ephesians 3:20*

As we trust and risk repeatedly, and with increasing measure, we grow to see God do great things through the Holy Spirit.

> *But you, dear friends, by building yourselves up in your most holy faith and praying in the Holy Spirit... –Jude 1:20*

Praying in the Spirit (in tongues) builds faith because you get used to feeling and sensing the spiritual world, rather than the world of the mind which is familiar and controllable. As prayer ministers, we need to cultivate our faith so we can see the miraculous when we pray. Then we are able to help those we pray for cultivate their own faith and take their own steps of risk.

QUESTIONS

1. How is your relationship with God? Is it as alive as you would like it to be?
2. Are you living as though dead? What desires, people, or plans in your life make it hard to stay that way?
3. Do you have others in your life who are resting in the branches of your faith? If not, what kinds of things could you do to grow your faith more?

ACTIVATION

Worship Encounter.

1. Play some quiet worship music.
2. Have everyone their eyes and put themselves in a posture of receiving. Don't say or think anything. Just receive.
3. Imagine God's unconditional love flowing toward you. Stay in this posture for a minute.
4. Then ask if He has anything to say to you. At the end, have anyone who is comfortable share what God did or said.

Sharing. Divide into micro groups.

1. Talk with the rest of the group about your relationship with God. If it is strong share your breakthrough moments and how you keep it strong. If it is weak, share your challenges.
2. Have each person tell a story from their own life when they made a decision by faith, as well as how God responded. If you don't have a big life event to share, you can always share how you got saved, how you got filled with the Spirit, or how you came to our Church.

If a ministry opportunity comes up, feel free to pray as the Holy Spirit leads.

STEPS YOU CAN TAKE

1. Make a list of what you are seeking in your life. Include things that take up your time and mental energies. Ask God which of these are from Him, and which He desires to reward. See if he gives you a Scripture for these things, or tells you something about them.
2. Get some resources around you, particularly for the goal of encouraging your faith. Find some things to read or listen to that are easy to pick up in the middle of the day, or in the middle of a crisis situation.

AUTHORITY

THE VICTORIOUS MINDSET

In order for us to be effective in ministry, we have to have God's perspective of ourselves and the battle we are in.

You are a Victor, Not a Victim

> *I will build my church, and the gates of hell shall not prevail against it.*
> *—Matthew 16:18*

The picture here is of a city under siege. But it isn't God's kingdom which is under siege! It is the devil's. We are besieging Satan's Kingdom, but it cannot stand against us. We're too strong for it. Much of the Church has had this idea backwards. We are afraid of the devil, when he is afraid of the church.

> *In all these things, we are **more than conquerors** through him who loved us. —*
> *Romans 8:37*

We are more than conquerors. We are victorious. Through Jesus and His love for us, we defeat every enemy. We need to reverse our image that much of Christian culture has given us. It might take a while to see victory, but just like the walls of Jericho, the devil's kingdom will fall.

> *The LORD will make you **the head, not the tail**. If you pay attention to the commands of the LORD your God that I give you this day and carefully follow them, **you will always be at the top, never at the bottom**.*
> *—Deuteronomy 28:13*

God doesn't want you getting beat up. He wants to give you authority over everything that holds you (or those you love) back. It doesn't matter whether you have "the gift" of healing, etc. Jesus has given you the authority and commission. You are kicking in the gates of hell.

> *For if, by the trespass of the one man, death reigned through that one man, how much more will those who receive God's abundant provision of grace and of the gift of righteousness **reign in life** through the one man. — Romans 5:17*

You are reigning in life through Christ. You are a living incarnation of the life of heaven. You represent His law and authority on earth, so the demons are supposed to quake—not you.

The Power Within You

> *You are of God, little children, and have overcome them, because greater is He who is in you than he who is in the world. —1 John 4:4*

We keep this within us when we pray. The Holy Spirit living inside of you is greater than any possible spiritual opposition you can encounter. We don't fear the devil, we make him fear.

> *Praise be to the LORD my Rock, who trains my hands for war, my fingers for battle. –Psalm 144:1*

God wants us to have a warrior mindset. He trains us for war so that we can win.

> *For the weapons of our warfare are not of the flesh but have divine power to destroy strongholds. – 2 Corinthians 10:4*

Our spiritual weapons have the power to destroy the power of Satan, and every stronghold that we besiege. The warrior mindset says we will fight until we see victory, no matter how long it takes.

Driving Out Fear

> *By his death he might break the power of him who holds the power of death— that is, the devil— and free those who all their lives were held in slavery by their fear of death. –Hebrews 2:14-15*

Fear is the door or the hook that the devil uses to keep us from walking in the authority God has given us. When we are afraid, it puts us in slavery to the devil. Jesus came to break fear so that we could have freedom and break the power of the devil.

> *There is no fear in love. But perfect love drives out fear. –1 John 4:18*

The reason why we're not afraid is because God says He is with us. If we are abiding in Jesus' perfect love, it drives out fear. It erodes false beliefs that put us into fear. If we are in fear, we're not in perfect love. It's the experience of God's perfect love that keeps us in peace. If it causes fear, it is not of God.

> *Behold, I have given **you** authority to tread on serpents and scorpions, and over all the power of the enemy, and nothing shall hurt you.*
> *– Luke 10:19*

In warfare, you may meet the enemy, but Jesus has defeated him so you do not have to fear. We do not think in terms of demonic attack, we think in terms of our own attack on God's behalf. We are given power over every form of opposition we can face. Nothing shall harm us. We should act like it.

> *No weapon that is formed against you shall prosper. – Isaiah 54:17*

We do not run from the battle, we run to the battle. Nothing the enemy can cook up will prosper against us. God is not keeping you into seasons of intense trial, He is trying to lead you out.

ACTIVATING YOUR AUTHORITY

Once we know who we are in Christ, we have to learn to walk in it. Faith without works is dead.

Your Kingdom Come

God handed his Kingdom over to Jesus, and then to believers. He initiated a siege on the devil's kingdom and the kingdoms of this world.

> *Your kingdom come, your will be done, on earth as it is in heaven.*
> *—Matthew 6:10*

In the Lord's prayer, He teaches us to pray for the Kingdom to come on earth. It has been said, "Most of us are busy thinking about getting off of the earth, but Jesus is trying to get on the earth." He wants and needs us here. There are still pockets of opposition. Our job is to bring His will and Kingdom here.

> *Nor will they say, 'Look, here it is!' or 'There!' for behold, the kingdom of God is in the midst of you. – Luke 17:21*

Some people have been taught to think of the Kingdom as future or as heaven, but the Kingdom is not a future event, it is a present reality.

The Source of Power

Because Jesus is in us, we are not limited in what we can do, just as He was not limited. We are all commanded and empowered to do everything Jesus did, because Jesus lives inside of us.

> *For you are all sons of God through faith in Christ Jesus. – Galatians 3:26*

> *In that day you will know that I am in my Father, and you in me, and I in you. – John 14:20*

Because we are in Christ, we have the authority of sons and daughters of God. Jesus' life shows us what that authority means.

> *I can do all things through Christ who strengthens me.—Philippians 4:13*

Take Authority

> *Proclaim as you go, saying, 'The kingdom of heaven is at hand.' Heal the sick, raise the dead, cleanse the lepers, cast out demons. Freely you have received, so freely give. – Matthew 10:7-8*

You don't need a special leading to tell the devil to go. A leading is helpful, but not necessary to accomplish God's will. God is in you, and has told you to do it, so you tell the devil to go. God's authority has been placed in you by God himself.

> And Moses said to the people, *"Fear not, stand firm, and see the salvation of the LORD, which he will work for you today. For the Egyptians whom you see today, you shall never see again. The LORD will fight for you, and you have only to be silent." The LORD said to Moses, "**Why do you cry to me?** Tell the people of Israel to go forward. Lift up **your** staff, and **stretch out your hand** over the sea and divide it, that the people of Israel may go through the sea on dry ground.*
> *–Exodus 14:13-15*

Moses gave them a sermon about what God would do, but then God gave Moses a sermon on what Moses was supposed to do. He and the Israelites were waiting on God, but God was waiting on them. Your hands are healing hands; your hands are hands of deliverance. Don't allow any sickness or weakness from disqualifying you because the authority is still within you to do what is necessary to get someone else free.

Speaking the Word

Living in a Kingdom mindset has practical application into how we minister. We have a mindset of cultivating our authority and commanding life.

> *That evening they brought to him many who were oppressed by demons, and he cast out the spirits **with a word** and healed all who were sick.*
> *–Matthew 8:16*

Jesus drove out evil spirits with a word. He also healed using commands.

> *Peter said, "I have no silver and gold, but what I do have I give to you. In the name of Jesus Christ of Nazareth, **rise up and walk**!" And he took him by the right hand and raised him up, and immediately his feet and ankles were made strong. –Acts 3:6-7*

The apostles followed this same pattern. We should not only pray, but we should use words to assert our authority over everything that opposes us.

> *The tongue has the power of life and death. –Proverbs 18:21*

What you say is very powerful. It has the power of life and death.

> *Look at the ships also: though they are so large and are driven by strong winds, they are guided by a very small rudder wherever the will of the pilot directs. So*

also the tongue is a small member, yet it boasts of great things. —James 3:4-5

The tongue has a rudder effect. Using words has the power of focusing our entire person on what we are saying. It has the ability to take control of our emotions and assert the truth of God. This is "confessing the Word," and is an effective tool for growing in the Lord especially when your mind gets off.

> *Jesus said to it, "May no one ever eat fruit from you again." … As they passed by in the morning, they saw the fig tree withered away to its roots. And Peter remembered and said to him, "Rabbi, look! The fig tree that you cursed has withered." And Jesus answered them, "Have faith in God. Truly, I say to you, whoever **says** to this mountain, 'Be taken up and thrown into the sea,' and does not doubt in his heart, but believes that **what he says will come to pass**, it will be done for him.*
> *—Mark 11:14,21-22*

Jesus promises that what we say will have power, even over the natural elements. As we grow in faith and unity with Christ, our words also grow in authority.

> *If you confess with your mouth that Jesus is Lord and believe in your heart that God raised him from the dead, you will be saved.*
> *—Romans 10:9*

It is not simply the act of speaking, but the combination of believing and speaking that leads to salvation (wholeness). It's an alignment of what you believe with what you say that creates the power. We never deny reality, but we declare a greater reality.

Be encouraged if things are happening, you are doing something! Speak the truth, and speak in tongues until whatever oppresses you is disciplined. Focusing on the devil only empowers him, but focusing on God and empowers him and brings his Kingdom in.

TONGUES

Speaking in tongues is a way we express our authority as believers over the flesh and over the spiritual powers of this world.

Speaking in Tongues

He who speaks in a tongue does not speak to men, but to God. No one understands him; he utters mysteries in the Spirit... −1 Corinthians 14:2

Speaking in tongues moves us out of the natural thoughts and into the realm of the Spirit.

*They saw what seemed to be tongues of fire that separated and came to rest on **each of them**. **All of them** were filled with the Holy Spirit and began to speak in other tongues as the Spirit enabled them. −Acts 2:3-4*

Speaking in tongues is not a gift for a chosen few, but an empowerment that is available to all believers.

The one who speaks in a tongue edifies himself...−1 Corinthians 14:4

Speaking in tongues is given to believers for the purpose of edifying yourself, or building yourself up, something God wants for all of His children.

And when Paul had laid his hands on them, the Holy Spirit came on them, and they began speaking in tongues and prophesying. − Acts 19:6

All of them were filled with the Holy Spirit and began to speak in other tongues as the Spirit enabled them. − Acts 2:4

When the Holy Spirit comes in Acts, speaking in tongues is often associated. Sometimes this is referred to as a "filling" of the Holy Spirit. While every believer has the Holy Spirit, we believe that God wants us all to experience his full working in and through us, including speaking in tongues.

*Settle it therefore in your minds not to meditate beforehand how to answer, for **I will give you words** and wisdom, which none of your adversaries will be able to withstand or contradict. − Luke 21:14-15*

Notice that speaking in tongues does not happen all on its own. It says **"They** began speaking..." In the same way that God gives us the words to speak by the Holy Spirit in our own language at the time we need them, he gives us words in tongues as we speak. One of the main reasons why people do not speak in tongues is that they expect God to jump on them and make them talk. The key is to begin speaking and He will give you the words.

The second reason people have trouble speaking in tongues, is that we are so conditioned to use our minds, that we expect understanding to come. But the Bible divorces praying with the Spirit and praying with the mind. Spiritual prayer bypasses what we know and what we don't know.

> *For if I pray in a tongue, my spirit prays, but my mind is unfruitful.*
> *–1 Corinthians 14:14*

Speaking in tongues is a gift received and experienced through faith, not intellect. This means you cannot expect to know what you are going to say in tongues, or in prophecy, in advance.

Why Speak in Tongues

> *I thank God that I speak in tongues more than all of you. – 1 Corinthians 14:18*

Being able to speak in tongues and actually doing it are the not the same thing. It's the difference between having a workout bench and using it.

> *But you, dear friends, by building yourselves up in your most holy faith and praying in the Holy Spirit... –Jude 1:20*

Speaking in tongues builds up your spirit. That's why it is good to do on a regular basis, especially in times that you feel spiritual oppression. Speaking in tongues combines the power of the spoken word, with faith.

> *In the same way, the Spirit helps us in our weakness. For we do not know how we ought to pray, but the Spirit Himself intercedes for us with groans too deep for words. And He who searches our hearts knows the mind of the Spirit, because the Spirit intercedes for the saints according to the will of God. – Romans 8:26-27*

The Spirit prays what is on God's mind. The good part about bypassing your own mind is that you can pray when you don't know what to pray, when you have no words or information, or when you have prayed about an issue a lot and the words feel stale.

Praying to Speak in Tongues

Speaking in tongues imparts spiritual strength, so when you sense that someone is spiritually weak, or living only from their mental faculties, it is a good time to ask them if they speak in tongues. Many times you will find they are able, but never actually do it. In this case, encourage them to do it more and with more confidence and force.

If they have never spoken in tongues, in keeping with our "naturally supernatural" philosophy, we want to use a low-key process that encourages but does not pressure them or make them feel uncomfortable. When you sense that someone is ready to speak in tongues, use a low-pressure procedure as below:

1. Ask the person if they have ever spoken in tongues and if they would like to be empowered to do so.
2. Lay hands on them and have them invite the Holy Spirit to come fill them and empower them to speaking in tongues. Remind them *that "Whatever you ask for in my name, I will do." –John 14:13.*
3. Agree with their prayer. You may pray in tongues in a low-key way to help them get started.
4. Encourage them to go ahead and try to speak in tongues. Some people hear a syllable, others don't. They key is to begin speaking. If nothing happens or they do not feel comfortable, don't add pressure. Tell them that it is very common for it to happen to privately after praying this way.

QUESTIONS

1. When you think about being victorious, and having authority, are there any theologies or beliefs that hold you back from that?
2. When a person needing ministry comes to you, do you feel confident that you can heal, deliver, or minister whatever they need? If not, why not?
3. Can you break the sense of oppression or attack, when it comes on? If so, how?

ACTIVATION

Share and Prayer. Break up into groups of 3 or 4 and tell each other about your experiences with speaking in tongues. Explain how you use tongues, confession, or other techniques in your devotional life. If one of you does not speak in tongues, and are open to receiving that gift, minister it to them using the model provided. Or you may wait until the end of the activation time to minister the Holy Spirit to someone together, as a whole group.

STEPS YOU CAN TAKE:

1. Practice speaking in tongues. Try to break through into a different level of intensity. Identify with the posture of a warrior and give yourself completely to it.
2. Mix in declarations of faith and authority with your speaking in tongues. Declare God's victory over your enemies, as well as over those you prayed for this week. Find some Scriptures on this topic that speak to you, to proclaim.

HEALING

GOD'S WILL FOR HEALING

This is the first hurdle that everyone must cross in order to be healed is knowing God wants to do it. He also wants us to exercise it. It's God's heart to both heal and heal through His children, the Body of Christ. You cannot exercise faith if you are not sure what God's will is.

Jesus Declares His Will

> *While Jesus was in one of the towns, a man came along who was covered with leprosy. When he saw Jesus, he fell with his face to the ground and begged him, "Lord, if you are willing, you can make me clean." Jesus reached out his hand and touched the man. "I am willing," he said. "Be clean!" And immediately the leprosy left him. – Mark 5:1-3*

A man with a contagious skin disease wanted to be healed, but was doubtful about whether or not Jesus would want to heal him. Jesus made God's will clear– "I am willing" – and then healed him.

> *"This is what you are to say to the Israelites: 'I AM has sent me to you.'"*
> *– Exodus 3:14*

God revealed Himself to Moses as the great "I Am." Jesus invoked this when He said "*I am* willing."

> *So Jesus said to them, "Truly, truly, I say to you, the Son can do nothing of his own accord, but only what he sees the Father doing. For whatever the Father does, that the Son does likewise. For the Father loves the Son and shows him all that he himself is doing. –John 5:19-20*

It's easy to forget that Jesus' ministry was the physical expression of the Father's will—neither He nor the Holy Spirit acts on their own. If it was Jesus' will to heal, we know it is also the Father's. He is a healing God.

God's Very Nature

> *I will not bring on you any of the diseases I brought on the Egyptians, for **I am the LORD, who heals you.** –Exodus 15:26*

In this Scripture, God identifies healing not just as something he does, but as who he *is.* Healing is part of his very nature.

> *Bless the LORD, O my soul,*

*and forget not **all** his benefits,*
*who forgives **all** your iniquities,*
*who heals **all your diseases**... –Psalm 103:2-3*

The psalmist was moved to praise God from his very being because he knew God's nature was redemptive, forgiving, and healing. They all went together.

And the LORD will take away from you all sickness, and none of the evil diseases of Egypt, which you knew, will he inflict on you.
– Deuteronomy 7:15

God promised in the Old Covenant to "take away all sickness." Notice there were no conditions on this. In fact, the implication is that at least some of the diseases he would heal were self-inflicted or culturally caused—"the evil diseases of Egypt." If the Old Covenant, which Israel could not fulfill, promised this, then how much more does the New Covenant, where Jesus has fulfilled the Old, promise health to us?

Jesus Healed All

*When evening came, they brought to Him many who were demon-possessed; and He cast out the spirits with a word, and **healed all who were ill**. – Matthew 8:16*

*Many followed Him, and **He healed them all**. – Matthew 12:15*

*And he went throughout all Galilee, teaching in their synagogues and proclaiming the gospel of the kingdom and **healing every disease** and **every affliction among the people**. So his fame spread throughout all **Syria**, and they brought him all the sick, those afflicted with various diseases and pains, those oppressed by demons, those having seizures, and paralytics, and he healed them. —Matthew 4:23-24*

These are just a few of the numerous verses in the New Testament which describe Jesus as healing **all** who were brought to him. He even healed people outside Israel and across the Jordan, in Gentile areas. No conditions. We can say with certainty that if Jesus were here in person, he would heal you and anyone you would bring to Him.

Healing in the Atonement

*Surely he **took up our pain and bore our suffering**, yet we considered him punished by God, stricken by him, and afflicted. But he was pierced for our*

transgressions, he was crushed for our iniquities; the punishment
*that brought us peace was on him, and **by his wounds we are healed**.*
–Isaiah 53:4-5

This famous passage about the Messiah promises that not only does Jesus come to forgive sins, but also to heal us.   He was wounded so that we could be healed.

In the atonement, we are healed because Jesus' sacrifice brought total healing in the spiritual and natural realms. The healing of our separation from God and restoration to Him spiritually has a visible expression in the healing of our bodies.

While they were eating, Jesus took bread, and when he had given thanks, he
broke it and gave it to his disciples, saying, "Take and eat; this is my body."
Then he took a cup, and when he had given thanks, he gave it to them,
saying, "Drink from it, all of you. This is my blood of the covenant, which is
poured out for many for the forgiveness of sins."
–Matthew 26:26-28

The communion is a meal of grace and a meal of healing. When we take the cup of communion, we drink the blood for forgiveness of sins, but the body which was "broken for us" (1 Corinthians 11:24), is for our physical bodies. The resurrection is life to our mortal bodies at the end of time, but the healing of our bodies is for now.

Believe God Wants It

And without faith it is impossible to please him, for whoever would draw near
to God must believe that he exists and that he rewards those who seek him. –
Hebrews 11:6

The essential features of any effective prayer also apply to praying for healing. We must believe that God wants to do it. You simply cannot get people healed praying, "If it be thy will..."

For we are members of his body, of his flesh, and of his bones.
–Ephesians 5:30

We are God's hand and feet on earth now. We have His nature within us because we partake of Him through communion and the Holy Spirit. He isn't physically here to heal people anymore, but we are!

ISSUES AND OBJECTIONS

The teaching of Scripture is very clear on healing, but our life experiences and preexisting theology can cause confusion or impede our belief in it.

"God's Timing"

> A woman who had **had a hemorrhage for twelve years**, and had endured much at the hands of many physicians, and had spent all that she had and was not helped at all, but rather had grown worse-- after hearing about Jesus, she came up in the crowd behind Him and touched His cloak. For she thought, "If I just touch His garments, I will get well." **Immediately the flow of her blood was dried up**; and she felt in her body that she was healed of her affliction. – Mark 5:25-29

This woman was sick and suffering for 12 years, but when she came in contact with Jesus she was immediately healed. Sometimes we attribute our lack of healing to "God's timing" but it is always God's perfect will to heal us "immediately."

> And behold, there was a woman who had had a disabling spirit for eighteen years. She was bent over and could not fully straighten herself. When Jesus saw her, **he called her over** and said to her, "Woman, you are freed from your disability." And he laid his hands on her, and **immediately** she was made straight, and she glorified God.

> But the ruler of the synagogue, indignant because Jesus had healed on the Sabbath, said to the people, "There are six days in which work ought to be done. Come on those days and be healed, and not on the Sabbath day." Then the Lord answered him, "You hypocrites! Does not each of you on the Sabbath untie his ox or his donkey from the manger and lead it away to water it? And ought not this woman, a daughter of Abraham whom **Satan bound** for eighteen years, be loosed from this bond on the Sabbath day?" –Luke 13:11-16

Jesus could easily have waited 24 hours to heal this woman, since it was the Sabbath. After all, she had already waited 18 years for her healing. Instead, He called her over to Him and healed her *immediately*. He compares her being healed to giving a drink to a thirsty animal–something that any humane person would do.

Jesus' proactive steps here should rework any pre-existing beliefs about our necessary steps to get healed, or waiting on His timing. Because we know He came to destroy the works of the devil (1 John 3:8), anytime we face something potentially life-stealing, we know that it is the devil who wants us to wait and suffer longer, not God.

Objections to Healing

Objection 1: God puts sickness on people at some places in the Bible.

When people are made sick in the OT, it is always as a direct consequence of sin, which is more merciful than death which is deserved. In the New Testament, however, we are offered forgiveness of sin. Sin and sickness are tied together in the spiritual condition of man. Nowhere in the New Testament do we see God putting sickness on anyone. However, if there is any question about whether a sickness was caused by sin, you can repent, be forgiven, and then expect God to heal you.

Objection 2: What about Paul's Thorn?

When you look more closely at this passage (2 Cor 12:7) the text makes clear that Paul is dealing with some kind of demon: "a thorn in the flesh was given to me, a messenger of Satan to trouble me." This demon was allowed to torment him because of his "surpassingly great revelations," which none of us have had.   In addition, he goes on in verse 10 to describe the kinds of torments he is experiencing but does not mention sickness: "weaknesses, in insults, in hardships, in persecutions, in difficulties..."

Objection 3: My friend had faith, but wasn't healed.

When faced with this situation, we have a choice between believing either God wanted healing that was not accomplished for reasons we don't fully understand, or that God did not want the healing for reasons we don't understand. Given these two choices, and the clear testimony of Scripture that God wants to heal all, without clear revelation from God on a certain situation, we just sometimes have to accept that we don't know why our prayers were not effective in a certain case.

Consider the Person You Are Praying For

> *Bartimaeus, a blind beggar, the son of Timaeus, was sitting by the*
> *roadside. And when he heard that it was Jesus of Nazareth, he began to cry out*
> *and say, "Jesus, Son of David, have mercy on me!" .... And Jesus said to*
> *him, "What do you want me to do for you?" And the blind man said to him,*
> *"Rabbi, let me recover my sight." –Mark 10:46-52*

In this story an obviously blind man is crying out loudly for Jesus. Jesus could easily just have healed him, but Jesus first asked him what he wanted. Maybe, as a beggar, what he really wanted was money. We only pray for people that want to be healed. We do not push people for healing who are not asking to be healed.

> *Then he touched their eyes, saying, "According to your faith be it done to you."*
> *–Matthew 9:29*

Being disabled, or caring for a family member that is disabled, is extremely difficult and taxing. People in these situations have often been prayed for many times without any apparent result. It is not uncommon for people to strengthen themselves by saying that the sickness is a blessing because their suffering helps them to rely on Jesus. We do not argue or condemn them. We come alongside and pray for them where they are, according to their faith and belief.

MODES OF HEALING

We see several different modes of healing in the Bible.

Commanding Healing

> *Then Jesus said to him, "Get up! Pick up your mat and walk." – John 5:8*

This is a typical case of Jesus healing someone in the New Testament. Jesus did not pray for the sick. He commanded them to be well. He did this because God had already given Him authority to heal them.

> *Heal the sick, and tell them, "The Kingdom of God is near you now."*
> *–Luke 10:9*

Jesus likewise gave this authority to the disciples. He did not instruct them to pray for the sick, but to heal them. It's the difference between asking your father to drive to the store, and driving to the store on your own. God has empowered you as his son or daughter to bring his will to the earth.

> *Heal the sick, raise the dead, cleanse those who have leprosy, drive out demons. Freely you have received; freely give. –Matthew 10:8*

You have been given permission by God to do His works, and even ordered to do so!

Releasing God's Presence

> *A woman in the crowd had suffered for twelve years with constant bleeding, and she could find no cure. Coming up behind Jesus, she touched the fringe of his robe. Immediately, the bleeding stopped. "Who touched me?" Jesus asked. Everyone denied it, and Peter said, "Master, this whole crowd is pressing up against you." But Jesus said, "Someone deliberately touched me, for **I felt healing power go out from me**."– Luke 8:46*

Jesus very presence is healing. Healing power went out from Jesus *without Him even commanding it*. When you pray for people, God's presence and power can flow directly from you into a person. Have faith that when you touch them, God can flow into them.

Healing by Revelation

> *And behold, some people brought to him a paralytic, lying on a bed. And when Jesus saw their faith, he said to the paralytic, "Take heart, my son; your sins are*

forgiven." And behold, some of the scribes said to them-selves, "This man is blaspheming." But Jesus, knowing their thoughts, said, "Why do you think evil in your hearts? For which is easier, to say, 'Your sins are forgiven,' or to say, 'Rise and walk'? But that you may know that the Son of Man has authority on earth to forgive sins"—he then said to the paralytic—"Rise, pick up your bed and go home." And he rose and went home. —Matthew 9:2-7

In this story, Jesus saw that the man felt guilty by prophetic revelation, so He forgave him. Then He read the thoughts of the Pharisees in by revelation. These two things released faith in the man to be healed.

God can use revelation through us in the same way. When you become aware of someone's sickness or inner pain by prophetic revelation, or otherwise get information about their life, God will often use this to release faith in both of you for healing. Or God may lead you to do something prophetic to encourage faith. Pray for healing in the "aha!" moment when their faith opens the door.

GETTING GOING

Once we know God's will for healing, we need to begin to step out and build our capacity to heal.

Believe In Yourself

If you have guilt, self-doubt, or other attitudes in your heart which cause you to believe that God can't or won't heal through you, you have to attack these before you'll see results. Otherwise if a healing doesn't happen, you'll just return to the negative attitudes instead of pressing forward in faith. Knowing your position as God's son or daughter is essential to faith. Similarly, don't make your healing record dependent on fasting, praying, or another prerequisite. This can become a trap and lead you doubt yourself rather than trust God.

Prime the Pump

You can "catch" faith for healing more easily than you can be taught it. This is how the disciples became strong in healing. They watched Jesus do it. Reading books on healing, listening to healing stories, watching YouTube clips on healing, are all important ways to build your faith. Just like everything else in life, watching someone else do it makes it seem much more possible. Once you know the truth, it's not about what these things teach you, but about the faith they release.

Try, Try, and Retry

Most people who are successful in healing give the testimony that they literally prayed for hundreds of people before they started to see any significant success. This does not mean you will have to pray for hundreds, but it means that if you give up after only a few, you are giving up way too soon.

> They came to Bethsaida, and some people brought a blind man and begged Jesus to touch him. He took the blind man by the hand and led him outside the village. When he had spit on the man's eyes and put his hands on him, Jesus asked, "Do you see anything?" He looked up and said, "I see people; they look like trees walking around." **Once more** Jesus put his hands on the man's eyes. Then his eyes were opened, his sight was restored, and he saw everything clearly. —Mark 8:22-24

Even Jesus prayed for healing more than once sometimes. During a single session, judge how much patience the person has to be prayed for multiple times. If they are willing to be prayed for several times, do so. Additionally, remember that it is now about *how* you pray or heal, but that you practice it.

Meditate on the Good

Finally, brothers, whatever is true, whatever is honorable, whatever is just, whatever is pure, whatever is lovely, whatever is commendable, if there is any excellence, if there is anything worthy of praise, think about these things. – Philippians 4:8

Meditating on failure produces failure. You have to focus on what God has done and wants to do more of, if you want to see more results. When you see someone healed or even make a slight improvement, thank God. Consider keeping a journal of your successes—even small ones—to encourage your faith.

Even when we think of "getting healed" we have a tendency to think of the negative condition—how bad it is—but hope Jesus can somehow make the positive win. Instead, we should think of Jesus' positive condition that overrides all negative conditions.

QUESTIONS

1. Do you have any issues that block your personal faith for healing? An approach you've been taught, or an especially difficult case?
2. What changes will you make regarding praying for healing, based on this teaching?
3. How will you personally handle discouragement if someone you pray for is not healed?

ACTIVATION

Tell Testimonies. Break into small groups and have each person tell a healing testimony they have, big or small. Be vulnerable about the process. This builds faith for the group.

Healing Prayer. Ask for anyone that needs physical healing among you. If anyone has something that is detectable and causing them pain at that time, start with that person. Ask them how much pain they feel on a scale of 1-10. Pray for them. Command that their body be healed. Ask them if it has changed. If it has, then thank God for the movement. Pray again if necessary. Repeat steps 2-6 as the person desires. If there are no obvious health issues among you, praise God and pray for the less obvious ones.

STEPS YOU CAN TAKE

1. Read some healing testimonies, or watch some videos of physical healing to build your faith. Several good options are:
    a. Paid in Full, Art Thomas (book or DVD documentary),
    b. John G. Lake, Complete teaching (book)
    c. Healing at Disneyland (YouTube)
    d. James Maloney healing clips (YouTube)
2. Pray for healing in your inner circle of family and friends, for as many issues that come up this week. Pray with the person, keeping it short, and repeating several times as appropriate.

THE PASTORAL PERSPECTIVE

A PASTOR'S VIEW OF LIFE

Your view of life has a big impact on how you minister. As you go through life with the Lord, you develop new perspectives which help you to navigate life better than before. Most pastors, who care for others professionally, gain additional insights. This session will give you some of the foundations of pastoral wisdom for you to minister from. A mature understanding of how God helps people will lead to mature prayer and prophetic ministry that changes people's lives.

Jesus is Your Pastor

"I am the Good Shepherd." – John 10:11

Jesus is your pastor. He is also the pastor of everyone you will pray for. Jesus pastors us and the lost with one goal: to bring everyone into close relationship with the Heavenly Father. When you are praying for someone, you should always remember that Jesus is the one doing the pastoring. Your job is to help the person connect to and hear Jesus. Our ultimate job is to come alongside the person we are ministering to and help them interact with Jesus more successfully. God has things he is trying to get the person to hear. They have things they are hoping God is hearing from them. We are facilitating that to work better. We are partnering in the pastoral process.

"Whoever has ears to hear let him hear." – Matthew 11:15

"I have much more to say to you, more than you can now bear."
– John 16:12

The primary challenge Jesus faces in leading us is our deafness and self-will. This is why He has to lead us one step at a time. As we obey Him step by step, He leads us out of our personal bondages. He can't give us everything we need all at once because we are unable to hear it. He reveals more as He transforms us more.

The disciples came to him and asked, "Why do you speak to the people in parables?" He replied, "Because the knowledge of the secrets of the kingdom of heaven has been given to you, but not to them... This is why I speak to them in parables: Though seeing, they do not see; though hearing, they do not hear or understand." – Matthew 13:10-11,13

Jesus spoke in parables because they did not have ears to hear or eyes to see. The parables were designed to open their hearts to give them the possibility of hearing and seeing the truth. He knew that if He spoke directly to them, they would shut down and reject the truth.

Likewise, when we minister, we must be careful about how direct we are, because it may have the effect of pushing someone away when God is drawing them. We also watch how much we share and try to narrow it to the pressing issue of the moment. The primary issue is how much someone can see or hear, and we help them see or hear at the level that they are able to.

God's Heart for You

> *"How often I have longed to gather your children together, as a hen gathers her chicks under her wings, and you were not willing."*
> *– Matthew 23:37*

God's desires for us are impossibly good. In fact they are better for you than your own desires for yourself. Our selfish desires hinder us and the good that God wants to give us. This is because what we want for ourselves is often tainted by ego, pleasure, or something that would ultimately be bad for us. On the other hand, some of us have desires for ourselves that are too low. What God wants for you is always better than what you yourself would accept.

> *For God did not send his Son into the world to condemn the world, but to save the world through him. – John 3:17*

When we minister to people on God's behalf, we look at them through the most redemptive lens, and dream for their lives together with God. We always participate with Jesus' saving plans. We never judge or look down on people even if their problems are severe. If they feel we are looking down on them, this can be extremely damaging in a prayer situation because their spirits are open and we represent the Lord.

God's redemptive plans allow us to make mistakes. Peter "messed up" multiple times during Jesus' life, but he still fulfilled the calling Jesus had for him. God's vision is always bigger, grander, more loving and restorative which means if a person is in front of you asking for prayer, God always wants to restore, repair, and redeem them. Within this, we avoid theologies about why they aren't receiving blessing. Instead, we look to minister in love to what's keeping them in a holding pattern.

Getting Out of the Wilderness

> *Then Jesus was led by the Spirit into the wilderness to be tempted by the devil. – Matthew 4:1*

One of the most popular theologies which stall God's will in a person's life is the "wilderness" theology. People believe they are in long seasons of difficulty for reasons such as God has put them there to learn a valuable lesson, or the devil has attacked them. But God always wants to lead people out of their wilderness seasons.

> It is eleven days' journey from Horeb by the way of Mount Seir to Kadesh-Barnea. —Deuteronomy 1:2

The Israelites wandered in the desert for forty years because of their unbelief and disobedience, but God's will was that they only be there for a week and a half! Even still, the Lord took care of their needs for food, water, and clothing. They experienced no lack because of His goodness towards them, even while they did not believe Him.

> Many are the afflictions of the righteous, but the Lord delivers him out of them all. — Psalm 34:19

Similarly, God wants you out of suffering and sickness. He doesn't promise that you won't experience them, but He does promise that He wants to lead you out.

When we pray, it is not our place to insert our opinions or explanations about why God might be withholding relief from someone—or confirm theirs. It is up to us to connect with the perfect will of God, and pray for that to come to earth as it is in heaven.

God Offers Us Choices

When we discover that someone can hear well from God, we have a tendency to treat them like a fortune teller than a conduit for a relationship. Prophecy is not fortune-telling, but a divine invitation to relationship and growth. Most things we see and say are contingent on the way the person lives and responds to God's leading. God offers us invitations and we respond.

> Forty more days and Nineveh will be overthrown. — Jonah 3:4

Jonah told Nineveh that God was going to overturn the city, but it did not happen because they repented. People interact with God in relationship. Our future is not predetermined.

Interpreting God's Work In Your Life

> You know how to interpret the appearance of the sky, but you cannot interpret the signs of the times. — Matthew 16:3

Interpreting God's working in your life is a skill of the mature Christian that many people have not developed yet. They cannot see what God is doing in their lives, and so the role of the prayer minister and pastor is to help them see what God is doing. We help them connect dots and give them understanding while we do that.

> *I tell you the truth, the Son can do nothing by himself. He does only what he sees the Father doing. Whatever the Father does, the Son also does.*
> *– John 5:19*

Even Jesus did not act on His own. He worked where He saw the Father at work. Likewise, we work where we see God at work. We help the person interpret the signs of God's activity and then we come alongside them and believe God with them.

Character Drives Your Life

> *But when you pray, go into your room, close the door and pray to your Father, who is unseen. Then your Father, who sees what is done in secret, will reward you.* — Matthew 6:6

Character—the invisible qualities of the heart—is what is determining your life. What you do during the regular part of your life, and especially in secret or when no one is looking, determines the opportunities that God opens up to you.

Sometimes people chase prophetic words as if they were magical, causal entities, but the real magic is what they are doing privately. Prophecy only helps accelerate and clarify whatever work is being done privately or in the invisible realm. *Character is always the context of prophecy*; prophecy is just the "brush strokes" on the real canvas. God is trying to pastor you and adjust who you are by using external voices, but you are at the helm and your character is the ship you're driving.

> *Then [Elisha] said, "Take the arrows," and the king [Jehoash] took them. Elisha told him, "Strike the ground." He struck it three times and stopped. The man of God was angry with him and said, "You should have struck the ground five or six times; then you would have defeated Aram and completely destroyed it. But now you will defeat it only three times.* —2 Kings 13:18-19

King Jehoash's prophetic opportunity to defeat Israel's enemies—which was God's will—was limited by his disobedience and lack of faith. Elisha opened the door to a great opportunity, but the character of the king determined how far it went. The principle at work is, every encounter with God involves a **process**. You have to do something, live into the encounter you had, and then stretch yourself into the dreams God has for you. Prayer and prophecy can create or surface new options, but the life process cannot be cut short simply by the announcement of a prophetic word. Character is king.

Death to Self

We are always at war between our fleshly desires and God's desires for us. God's process of pastoring us leads us to continually die to ourselves.

> *Whoever finds their life will lose it, and whoever loses their life for my sake will find it.* — Matthew 10:39

> *Whoever wants to be my disciple must deny themselves and take up their cross daily and follow me.* — Luke 9:23

Following Jesus is a process of continual denial of selfish goals in favor of selfless, love-driven goals. When we die to ourselves, our future accelerates. When we live for ourselves, our relationship with God and impact on the world reduce. In the Body of Christ, people are all along this spectrum; at any given moment, they are either moving more towards living for God or more towards living for themselves.

> *"All authority in heaven and on earth has been given to me. Therefore go and make disciples of all nations…"* –Matthew 28:18-19

God is in a war with the devil to reclaim his lost children. He saved you, so he wants you to participate and win the war. All true godly purposes come from our submission to God's bigger plan.

> *Many are the plans in a person's heart, but it is the LORD's purpose that prevails.* –Proverbs 19:21

We have to commit ourselves to God's plans to discover his plans for us. If you are praying for someone and you sense that they are not surrendered to God, then the plans they have will not prosper whether you pray for it or not. God may lead you to confront their need to surrender directly, or you might pray in a way that will permit God to reveal it to the person.

God Wants to Speak to the Root

> *Do people pick grapes from thorn bushes, or figs from thistles? Likewise, every good tree bears good fruit, but a bad tree bears bad fruit. A good tree cannot bear bad fruit, and a bad tree cannot bear good fruit.* – Matthew 3:10

Issues that people can see are usually manifestations of issues that they cannot see, but God can. You should always look beyond the visible and partner with God to see the invisible, where the root of the problem lies. We listen to the problem presented but always want to discern, "What is the problem behind the problem?"

> *James and John, the sons of Zebedee, came up to him and said to him, "Teacher, **we want you to do for us whatever we ask of you**." And he said to them, "What do you want me to do for you?" And they said to him, "Grant us to sit, one at your right hand and one at your left, in your glory." Jesus said to them, "You do not know what you are asking."*
> –Mark 10:35-38

Idols or bondages can block our embracing of God at certain spots. As prayer ministers, if we get a sense that the root of a problem is an idol or bondage, we should be careful not to prophesy about that but instead bring this out without making a person feel bad or anxious.

Sometimes people are more ashamed of the issue that you can see, than the ones you can't. This is often the case with a more "embarrassing" sin such as pornography or divorce. While people may feel condemned if you speak to these, as fruits of their life, they may welcome you speaking to roots such as anger or fear. It is good to ask questions gently which might lead you to being able to pray for these to be healed.

QUESTIONS

1. Have you ever given or received a word that you know was tainted by bad theology? What was the result?
2. Have you had the experience of God trying to tell you something important, for a long time? If a prophetic person could have spoken into your life about that, how could they have done it so you would have heard it?
3. Are you rock solid on the premise that God is always good and the devil is always bad? Are there any ministry situations you've had that have caused you to question this?
4. If someone gave you a word, would you view it as deterministic—like it would necessarily come to pass? Or magical—like blessings would just drop out of the air? Are you pursuing your character and overall life path in a way that will accelerate whatever prophecies you receive?

ACTIVATION

Pastoral Prayer. Divide into two or three smaller groups. Have one person describe the overall situation of their life and then take turns offering an interpretation of their situation based on the principles we discussed:

- God's love and desire to lead you to good things
- The possibility of choice
- Our need to die to our own desires and follow Him
- Speak to the root not the fruit

If there is time, go around to someone else in the circle.

STEPS YOU CAN TAKE:

1. Collect any prophetic words you have received in a certain place and review them. Ask God which parts apply to your life right now and decide on a step or two that could actualize them further.
2. Review some of Jesus' ministry situations in the gospels from the pastoral perspective lens. Note what things He discerned prophetically, which He decided to reveal, and how He chose to reveal them.

INNER HEALING & DELIVERANCE

HOW THE HUMAN PERSON IS FORMED

| Experiences | → | Emotions | → | Thoughts | → | Actions |

- ➢ **Experiences:** Our brains begin to be shaped from childhood by our experiences.
- ➢ **Emotions:** These experiences trigger emotions.
- ➢ **Thoughts:** These lead to thoughts and ideas.
- ➢ **Actions:** Our thoughts lead us to take actions.

Our identity begins with experiences and how we respond to them, resulting ultimately in action. However, in it's not a strict procedure, all of these components act in an interlocking fashion. New experiences are interpreted by the thoughts you have developed. These thoughts and interpretations lead to feelings. Our thoughts and feelings lead us to take actions or not.

In addition, this is not a closed system. External actors: people, God and the devil all influence the system, and ultimately, you make the choice on how to respond to it.

How You are Wired

When you are born, your brain is just developing, and so patterns are very flexible. As your parents, other primary care givers, and social groups respond and interact with you, these patterns become entrenched. You begin to develop beliefs about your identity, what kind of person you are.

> *For if you live according to the flesh, you will die; but if by the Spirit you put to death the misdeeds of the body, you will live. – Romans 8:13*

Even if we were born into Christian families, no matter how good our parents were, or how obedient we tried to be as children, we all develop patterns which are not healthy. They reflect our flesh, rather than the Spirit of God. Growth is the process of moving away from the flesh and toward the Spirit.

Instant vs. Progressive Freedom

> *"The kingdom of heaven is like a man who sowed good seed in his field. But while everyone was sleeping, his enemy came and sowed weeds among the wheat, and went away. When the wheat sprouted and formed heads, then the weeds also appeared. "The owner's servants came to him and said, 'Sir, didn't*

you sow good seed in your field? Where then did the weeds come from?' "'An enemy did this,' he replied."
– Matthew 13:24-28

Like weeds, many of our wounds are unintentionally planted while God is in the process of growing us. If a wound is like a weed in your heart, sometimes the simple removal of the weed is enough. Other times, the weed has spread through the whole garden and will require extensive ministry over a period of time.

Surprisingly, some of the most traumatic experiences can have the greatest results in a single setting. For example, if someone turned to drugs because they were hated and developed a false portrait of themselves, when they then discover there is a God who loves them, this new reality may overturn long held beliefs in an instant. Sometimes a power encounter is all that is necessary.

However, most of the issues that people struggle with, or come to receive pray for, are much deeper. They require continual detangling and loosening of the chains. When a person has tried the basics and is stuck, it is often because the kind of change they need will take time. Their identity was formed by a pattern that began at a certain time and has repeated over and over again throughout their lifetime. A new identity will only take root as they believe and experience the truth over and over. When these wounds happen early enough in life, it's a like a tree that is bent near the bottom. The tree grows up, but its shape is warped.

Focus on Jesus

Inner Healing and deliverance sometimes develop a focus on esoteric topics such as cursed objects, curses spoken over you, generational curses, Freemasonry, occultic experiences, or events that predate the person's memory. Jesus should be our focus and most of the time, these are a distraction. In the normal situation, simply bringing the issue to the surface, repenting and inviting Jesus into the situation will resolve it. If the Holy Spirit brings something more esoteric to the forefront, you can engage a trained minister in specialized ministry.

THE INNER HEALING PROCESS

Inner healing is a special kind of prayer that recognizes the role that these formative experiences and hidden beliefs play in shaping your everyday behavior. There are many different variations on how to do it, but they all have two key elements: bringing the issue to the surface, and bringing Jesus into the situation. We act as facilitators for the Holy Spirit to do the work.

Surfacing the Issue

We are not always aware of the things that are holding us back. They can lurk outside of our normal awareness. Sometimes, like a splinter that was never removed, the body has healed or grown over it, even though the splinter is still there and can cause pain when touched. Safety and compassion are the first conditions for someone to bring an issue to the surface. ***The safer they feel with you, the deeper God can go*** in bringing things to the surface.

Some people have believed it will hurt too much to bring up a past memory, so they have gone on without processing the pain—they may be afraid of "going back there." We don't want them to relive a situation. We ask the Holy Spirit to bring up or make known memories/false beliefs so they can be healed. This is like Him gently drawing up the splinter to the surface.

Invite Jesus into the Situation

Every problem anyone could ever have is the result of God not being present. When God is present, he protects, comforts and heals. Once someone has brought the point of pain to the surface, God can heal it.

- If the point of pain has to do with a sin they committed, or a false belief, lead them to repent and receive His forgiveness and grace. This should be done gently. If they are having trouble praying or finding the right words, you can lead them through a simple prayer of repentance and have them repeat after you. God wants to correct any wrong understanding of Him they may have, and apply love and forgiveness where it may be missing.
- If their point of pain has to do with a traumatic experience or being sinned against, first lead them through forgiving anyone involved. Again, you may supply them with words in prayer if they are having trouble, but it is important that they actually say them aloud because many people experience deliverance just through that process.
- It can be beneficial during prayer to ask Jesus to show them where He was at the moment of trouble in the past. Allowing them to visualize Jesus being there—or inserting Him into that painful memory—and then picturing Him

showing them the kindness they needed in those moments can often release a person's healing.

- Your final step is to have them ask Jesus to take away the pain and emotions associated with that situation and replace them with His love. Jesus is the healer, so the goal is to bring someone into the loving presence of Jesus. As you are able to remove the obstacles blocking the person from Jesus and his love, they will receive healing.

Start at the Beginning and Move Forward

Life controlling issues are not all simply rooted in one experience. The experience arises form an environment, and then creates a way of living that can foster new damaging experiences.

Since wounds and false beliefs follow a pattern which usually begins at an early age, it can be beneficial to take someone through a journey beginning with their earliest memory of that struggle or experience. Those traumas can hold the bondage in place. Dealing with each one is like removing a tent peg. Over time, you can repeat the healing process at each touchpoint all the way up to the present, and then focus on the present. What false beliefs are still guiding the person's behaviors now?

DELIVERANCE

When evening came, many who were demon-possessed were brought to Jesus,
and He drove out the spirits with a word and healed all the sick.
–Matthew 8:16

One of Satan's greatest strategies has been to scare people off from confronting him, out of fear or disgust. It is common for people to be freaked out about deliverance ministry because of stories they have heard or pop culture references they have been exposed to. We may be turned off completely or intimidated, thinking deliverance is hard and only for the specifically gifted. All this is from the enemy so that we will not counter him. In reality, Jesus accepted no intimidation from Satan..

Deliverance is for You

He said to them, "Go into all the world and preach the gospel to all creation…
And these signs will accompany those who believe: In my name they will drive
out demons – Mark 16:15,17

Jesus gives authority over demons to all of His disciples. It is therefore part of our mission here on earth.

The seventy-two returned with joy, saying, "Lord, even the demons are subject
to us in your name!" –Luke 10:17

Jesus has given you the power to deliver others from demons, and they must submit to you. They may resist, scream and shout, but they must submit when you stand your ground. As the disciples found out, the more you do it, the more respect and obedience you will get.

Relationship to Inner Healing

When an impure spirit comes out of a person, it goes through arid places
seeking rest and does not find it. Then it says, 'I will return to the house I
left.' When it arrives, it finds the house swept clean and put in order. Then it
goes and takes seven other spirits more wicked than itself, and they go in and
live there. –Luke 11:24-26

Inner healing and deliverance are very closely related. When something is broken in our hearts, a demon can enter that place. Once it enters that place, it makes things significantly worse because the demonic personality is evil. When we agree with it, our hearts become broken more deeply. On the other hand, when we close the door to the devil by repentance and faith, we are able to sweep the house of our heart clean.

Practically speaking, we pursue inner healing (sweeping the house), and if there happens to be a demon involved we will encounter it and drive it out.

Severe Cases

> *When Jesus got out of the boat, a man with an impure spirit came from the tombs to meet him. This man lived in the tombs, and no one could bind him anymore, not even with a chain. – Mark 5:2-3*

This man had lost complete control of himself and his identity. When we think of demons, this is normally what we think of. It's also something we're very unlikely to encounter in day to day ministry. In our society, people like this are normally put into a psychiatric ward. While every believer has authority over demons, Christians who deal with this kind of severe demonic oppression usually have a specialized ministry that they have developed over years.

Besides the most severe cases, there are several different kinds of demonic situations that pop up in the New Testament which we may see.

Standard Case

> *When the Sabbath day came, he went into the synagogue and began to teach. Suddenly, a man in the synagogue who was possessed by an evil spirit cried out. But Jesus reprimanded him. "Be quiet! Come out of the man," he ordered. At that, the evil spirit screamed, threw the man into a convulsion, and then came out of him. –Mark 1:21,23,25*

Once when Jesus was ministering, a demon manifested in someone who was otherwise apparently in their right mind. These are the cases we are most likely to encounter. The person may have no knowledge that there is a demon at work, and it may simply manifest while we are ministering to them. If it gets exposed, then we have the authority to quiet it and remove it.

> *Then a demon-possessed man who was blind and mute was brought to Jesus, and He healed the man so that he could speak and see. –Matthew 12:22*

Not all deliverances are dramatic. Because of the hype surrounding the demonic, you may encounter a person seeking ministry who assumes that their deliverance process will be loud and messy and projects that upon you as the minister. As a rule, we do not encourage this. While we recognize that manifestations sometimes do occur, likely due to spiritual confrontation—demons fighting the truth and authority of Jesus—we minimize manifestations or the expectation of them. There is no need to allow Satan to show off or take revenge on a person on the way out. He does not need any more attention. We simply magnify Jesus, and allow that to permeate a person so much that they become clean. For the purpose of ministry, if things do get dramatic, take the person to a side room, where you can continue the process.

Demonic Sickness

And there was a woman who for eighteen years had had a sickness caused by a spirit; and she was bent double, and could not straighten up at all. —Luke 13:11

There are several instances where the New Testament makes clear that a physical sickness was caused by a demon. The most obvious cases of demonic illness are ones that cannot be diagnosed by a doctor. These kinds of non-descript problems often cause pain and move around but cannot really be attributed to any cause. Knowing you are dealing with a demon in these cases can help you pray for healing more effectively.

And when Jesus saw that a crowd came running together, he rebuked the unclean spirit, saying to it, "You mute and deaf spirit, I command you, come out of him and never enter him again." —Mark 9:25

Jesus commanded an evil to come out the epileptic boy, leading us to understand that sometimes natural diseases are being held in place by a demonic force.

Coming out of Agreement

"When the unclean spirit has gone out of a person, it passes through waterless places seeking rest, but finds none. Then it says, 'I will return to my house from which I came.' And when it comes, it finds the house empty, swept, and put in order. Then it goes and brings with it seven other spirits more evil than itself, and they enter and dwell there, and the last state of that person is worse than the first. –Matthew 12:43-45

Before we command things to leave, we should ensure that the person is not in agreement with the demonic spirit they are hosting, or it will come right back.

Jesus replied, "Very truly I tell you, everyone who sins is a slave to sin." —John 8:34

When we sin, it puts us in a position of slavery. The evil one, who is the father of sin, becomes master. All life-besetting issues have some level of demonic involvement, even if we do not see it in an obvious way. Freedom from sin and freedom from Satan are closely intertwined.

> *"You will not certainly die," the serpent said to the woman. "For God knows that when you eat from it your eyes will be opened, and you will be like God, knowing good and evil." When the woman saw that the fruit of the tree was good for food and pleasing to the eye, and also desirable for gaining wisdom, she took some and ate it —Genesis 3:4-6*

Eve plunged the whole world into sin and death by agreeing with and taking action on a lie that Satan had told her. The devil has access by permission, and that permission is given by taking the bait of the lie, which may be associated with something attractive and desirable as it was for Eve, or it may be a discouraging lie the person believes about themselves.

> *Now repent of your sins and turn to God, so that your sins may be wiped away. —Acts 3;19*

> *For he has rescued us from the dominion of darkness and brought us into the kingdom of the Son he loves, —Colossians 1:13*

When we repent of our sins, God forgives them, and that transfers authority back from the Kingdom of darkness to the Kingdom of light.

Basic Process

> *if you confess with your mouth that Jesus is Lord and believe in your heart that God raised him from the dead, you will be saved. – Romans 10:9*

Repentance and confession are all we need to access Jesus power of salvation and deliverance. Therefore, when we are dealing with a Christian who wants deliverance, the process is a matter of removing the access point and then commanding the Spirit to go.

1. Have the person confess (admit) and repent of any agreement or underlying sin that the person has with that spirit.
2. Once they are done, command it to leave.
3. Ask them if they felt it lift. If not, repeat the above steps, until you get at the root.

Getting the "agreement" removed is the tricky part. Many people want freedom from the consequences but not freedom from the pleasures of the spirit they are hosting. We have to be willing to turn away from the pleasure as well as the lies associated with that spirit.

This agreement may also be present through a past wound or trauma, which needs to be dealt with. This allows wrong beliefs to take hold. Follow the Inner Healing process to deal with past wounds and the associated false beliefs.

QUESTIONS

1. What are your underlying assumptions about inner healing and deliverance, and who helped form those? How do you feel about the role that God, the devil, and a person's own wiring and character play?
2. Are you the kind of person that someone needing inner healing would come to? How about deliverance? If not, what kinds of things do you need to change to become that person?
3. What is your experience with inner healing and deliverance personally? What resources or processes have worked for you (or someone close to you)?

ACTIVATION

Pray for Inner Healing. Divide into gender separated small groups.

1. Ask someone who struggles with any recurring issue or thought pattern to share what they struggle with.
1. Ask the Holy Spirit for a memory related to that issue.
2. Ask Jesus to reveal Himself in the memory.
3. Have the person pray forgiveness and repentance as appropriate.
    a. If the point of pain has to do with a sin committed, or a false belief, have them repent and receive Jesus' forgiveness and grace.
    b. If it has to do with trauma or being sinned against, have them forgive the other person and ask Jesus to take away the pain and emotions associated with that situation and replace them with His love.
4. Have them come out of agreement with the enemy and into agreement with the Lord.
5. Command any demonic influence to go!
6. Pray restoration and blessing.

Pray until appropriate ministry is finished. Repeat with someone else if there is time.

STEPS YOU CAN TAKE

1. Familiarize yourself with some of the more popular inner healing resources and curriculum out there, including Celebrate Recovery and our church freedom group.
2. Research online some of the basic support groups available for common ministry situations, i.e. depression/anxiety, alcohol addiction, sexual addiction, domestic abuse.
3. Read a book on counseling and inner healing.

HEARING GOD FOR YOURSELF

UNDERSTANDING HOW GOD SPEAKS

Hearing God is foundational to having a relationship with Him. Because we minister out of relationship, it is important that we cultivate relationship.

Walking through our own troubles and decision-making with God, gives us a better perspective on what it is like for others we advise. We also will have a fruitful life and be connected to the One who is our source.

Jesus Promises It

*My sheep **hear My voice**, and I know them, and they follow Me.*
–John 10:27

*Call to me and **I will answer you**, and will tell you great and hidden things that you have not known. –Jeremiah 33:3*

Jesus promises that we will hear His voice. This is not just something for super-spiritual people. Conversation is a normal part of any relationship. It's very important that we develop the skill of listening, hearing, and following the living words of Jesus.

*"Man shall not live by bread alone, but by every word that **proceeds** from the mouth of God." –Matthew 4:4*

The Bible does not say that we live by the words that God spoke in the past tense, but the words that God is speaking in the present tense. What the Holy Spirit is saying to you now will give you life and make your life fruitful.

What God's Voice Is

*Then He said, "Go out, and stand on the mountain before the Lord." And behold, the Lord passed by, and a great and strong wind tore into the mountains and broke the rocks in pieces before the Lord, but the Lord was not in the wind; and after the wind an earthquake, but the Lord was not in the earthquake; and after the earthquake a fire, but the Lord was not in the fire; and after the fire a **still small voice**. So it was, when **Elijah heard it**, that he wrapped his face in his mantle and went out and stood in the entrance of the cave. Suddenly a voice came to him, and said, "What are you doing here, Elijah?" –1 Kings 19:11-13*

Sometimes we are looking for dramatic encounter, and that causes us to miss God's voice or His activity. God's normal mode of communicating with us is on the edge of our perception. Our soul must be quiet in order to hear Him.

"Hear my words: If there is a prophet among you, I the LORD make myself known to him in a vision; I speak with him in a dream. Not so with my servant Moses. He is faithful in all my house. With him I speak mouth to mouth, clearly, and not in riddles. —Numbers 12:6-8

God's voice is not always a "voice." He speaks to us in many different ways: dreams, visions, riddles, etc. As believers who are united with Him, the most basic form of hearing God is an idea. At first you may not recognize that they are God's ideas, but as you see the fruit, you will recognize them.

Listen to advice and accept instruction, that you may gain wisdom in the future. Many are the plans in the mind of a man, but it is the purpose of the LORD that will stand. – Proverbs 19:20-21

God also speaks through friends. You should listen for God's voice in the voice of others.

Now after Jesus was born in Bethlehem of Judea in the days of Herod the king, behold, wise men from the east came to Jerusalem, saying, "Where is he who has been born king of the Jews? For we saw his star when it rose and have come to worship him. —Matthew 2:1-2

God also speaks through "signs" or unusual circumstances that clue us to the fact that He is working. We should pay attention to the road signs in our lives and in those we minister to.

What God's Voice Isn't

Take my yoke upon you, and learn from me, for I am gentle and lowly in heart, and you will find rest for your souls. —Matthew 11:29

Jesus' voice sounds like Him. If you have a wrong idea of His character, it will be hard to discern Him properly. He is gentle and humble. He is not super-demanding and bossy. He invites us to the joy of following.

*Once when we were going to the place of prayer, we were met by a female **slave** who had a spirit by which she predicted the future. She earned a great deal of money for her owners by fortune-telling. She followed Paul and the rest of us, shouting, "These men are servants of the Most High God, who are telling you the way to be saved." She kept this up for many days. Finally Paul became so annoyed that he turned around and said to the spirit, "In the name of Jesus Christ I command you to come out of her!" At that moment, the spirit left her. – Acts 16:16-18*

By contrast, the devil shouts and speaks all the time, trying to drown out your identity and the voice of the Lord, but God speaks inside of you in the whisper.

Playing the God Card

Some people are fond of telling everyone that "God told me…" for pretty much everything they do. This can be discouraging and make you feel like you are not hearing God at all.

> But as many as received him, to them He gave power to become the **sons** of God, even to them that believe on His name… –John 1:12

If God told you what to do you every second, He would be controlling you, rather leading you in relationship. He has called you as a son or daughter, not a slave. This applies to how we minister as well. Part of us being "naturally supernatural" is that we don't play the "God card." We encourage one other by being humble about what we think we are hearing, and we are transparent about when we don't hear anything or don't hear correctly.

What Makes it Hard

> He who has ears to hear, let him hear. – Matthew 11:15

Jesus spoke in parables because people are naturally hard of hearing. Some things we would block out if we were told directly. This is why Jesus told people indirectly, so that the truth would "seep in."

> The wind blows wherever it pleases. You hear its sound, but you cannot tell where it comes from or where it is going. So it is with everyone born of the Spirit." –John 3:8

We must be open to whatever God wants to say. This is not just a mental state, it's also a condition of the heart. We become open to being led. We begin to enjoy the chase, realizing that God's direction is the most exciting and fulfilling.

> "Why do you look at the speck of sawdust in your brother's eye and pay no attention to the plank in your own eye? How can you say to your brother, 'Let me take the speck out of your eye,' when all the time there is a plank in your own eye? –Matthew 7:3-4

Hearing God for yourself and hearing God for others are different skills in the same way that removing a speck from your own eye versus someone else's is. Some of us may have **particular areas** where it is hard for us to hear God because we have an idea or attachment in that specific area that blocks us. In fact, it is often the case that what we need to hear most is the hardest for us to hear.

"But whoever should drink from the water which I will give him— he will never thirst, ever. On the contrary, the water which I will give him will become a spring of water in him, bubbling-up to eternal life."
–John 4:14

The river of God's life comes from within us. Because you are united with God, God's thoughts and your thoughts become intertwined. You are not always completely sure who is who—and you don't always have to be. When you are completely submitted to Him and following Him, it doesn't really matter because you and He are one; His will will be accomplished.

PRACTICAL STEPS TO HEARING GOD

Paying attention to God is a big part of hearing him better. Several methods work to bring attention to His voice and get better at discerning it.

Developing the Right Heart Posture

> *Then the man and his wife heard the sound of the Lord God as he was walking in the garden in the cool of the day, and they hid from the Lord God among the trees of the garden. But the Lord God called to the man, "Where are you?" – Genesis 3:8-9*

God is always pushing the envelope in the relationship. We often think our walk with God all rides on us, but God reached out to us before we knew Him. He still takes the first step. When we're seeking to hear God's voice for ourselves, we don't have to strive, we have to yield.

> *Let us then approach God's throne of grace with confidence, so that we may receive mercy and find grace to help us in our time of need.*
> *–Hebrews 4:16*

> *Draw near to God and he will draw near to you. –James 4:8*

Believing that nothing is barring you from God, from His perspective, will help you develop a place of communion that you can hear His voice in, whether for yourself or others. Ask these questions to help your heart to be postured correctly:

➢ Do you have the confidence that God is always with you?
➢ Do you know that He is always for you?
➢ Do you know He always wants to come closer and closer to you?
➢ Do you know that God is not holding out on you?

Tune In

For now we see in a mirror dimly, but then face to face. Now I know in part;
then I shall know fully, even as I have been fully known.
—1 Corinthians 13:12

Although we see dimly here from earth, we can see more clearly as we seek Him. Living a lifestyle of hearing means turning down the other things we are listening to: YouTube, Facebook, Netflix, games, etc. Spend time in quiet instead. It is important to spend time "polishing the mirror."

Practice Makes Perfect

"I will bring you back to the land of Israel. Then you, my people, will know that I
am the LORD, when I open your graves and bring you up from them. I will put
my Spirit in you and you will live, and I will settle you in your own land. Then you
will know that I the LORD have spoken, and I have done it," declares the LORD.
—Ezekiel 37:12-14

God tells the people of Israel that they will know that He has spoken *after* it has come to pass. By paying attention to whether something we hear happens or not, we can learn to discern God's voice better. It's like a tuning process.

The Lord is not slow to fulfill his promise as some count slowness, but is patient
toward you. —2 Peter 3:9

Some people are fond of saying that "delayed obedience is disobedience," which puts a very negative spin onto something very positive. Following the invisible God is a journey we learn more of, as we do it. We don't always get it right the first time. God gives us many chances to get out of our mess.

Journaling

This is what the LORD, the God of Israel, says: "Write down for the record
everything I have said to you, Jeremiah." —Jeremiah 30:2

Journaling is a very effective way to develop your ability to hear God's voice, because it helps you be clear about what you heard. Start by keeping a log of what God has said to you and done through you. Meditate on these things and review them, as they will build your faith. They will also clue you in on how God typically speaks to you—key words, key subjects, using your name, using Scripture, etc. A good exercise to break open your flow is to write a letter from God to you. Think about His character and His love for you, and try to imagine what He would say. Many times this will be close to what He actually would say.

Get Mentoring

"But what about you?" he asked. "Who do you say I am?" Simon Peter
answered, "You are the Messiah, the Son of the living God." Jesus
replied, "Blessed are you, Simon son of Jonah, for this was not revealed to you
by flesh and blood, but by my Father in heaven...Peter took him aside and
began to rebuke him. "Never, Lord!" he said. "This shall never happen to you!"
But he turned and said to Peter, "Get behind me, Satan! You are a hindrance to
me. For you are not setting your mind on the things of God, but on the things of
man."
–Matthew 16:15-17; 22-23

Peter did not know how to recognize the voice of God on His own yet, even though he *was* hearing it. Jesus, who heard very well, gave him coaching on which voices he was hearing. One of "his" thoughts was actually God's voice, and one of "his" thoughts was actually Satan's voice. Jesus giving him clear direction helped him to learn the voice of God.

The Western education system is highly based on book learning, but many things are not best learned from a book. If you wanted to learn how to play tennis, would you get a book about it? Consider finding a coach who has worked through hearing God's voice well.

ACTIVATION

Sharing Time. Split into two groups and have a roundtable discussion about hearing God. Have each person share for 3-5 minutes about where they are on their journey of hearing God. Ask them one or more of the following questions:

1. Is it easy or hard for you to hear God's voice? Why is it that way? Share any special ways that work for you, or challenges you have had.
2. Do you have any stories of hearing God's voice that especially stand out in your life? What did you learn from that?
3. What do you do to help the process of "polishing the glass" in your own life, or what have you done recently that worked?
4. What is your experience with people playing "the God card" in prayer ministry? Is there anything you need to change, or have been working on changing in this area?

As the Holy Spirit leads, pray or minister to anyone in your group who may need it, regarding this topic and their experiences.

STEPS YOU CAN TAKE:

1. Consider a good friend or mentor for you, to help you take the next step in hearing God's voice for yourself better.
2. Get a good book or resource on hearing God's voice.
3. Start an encounter journal that would include things like:
   - Anything God says to you.
   - Anything God says through you.
   - Things you pray over someone else that resonate with them.
   - Things someone else prays over you that resonate with you.
   - Dreams or visions God gives you.
   - Anything else that God does for you.

   At the end of the week, review how God is working in your life.

HOW TO GET PROPHETIC REVELATION

OVERVIEW OF PROPHECY

Prophetic ministry is one of the most powerful ways we can encounter and relate to God on this side of heaven. As a prayer minister, we want everyone to grow in their ability to touch lives through healthy prophetic ministry.

All May Prophesy

> For **you can all prophesy** one by one, so that all may learn and all be encouraged.   −1 Corinthians 14:31

Everyone has the ability to prophesy, even though some are more developed than others and some have greater gifts than others. Prophecy is not for a chosen few while others watch. This "spectator sport" perspective is what makes man marvel at man—the exact opposite of what the New Testament teaches prophecy is about.

Why We Prophesy

> But the one who prophesies speaks **to people** for their **strengthening, encouraging and comfort.** − 1 Corinthians 14:3

The purpose of NT prophecy is not fortune-telling or doom and gloom warnings about End Times events. It is to strengthen, encourage and comfort other believers. Sometimes God gives us something challenging to say, but His purpose is always positive.

Kinds of Prophecy

> For to one is given the word of wisdom through the Spirit, and to another the word of knowledge according to the same Spirit... and to another prophecy. −1 Corinthians 12:8,10

When we speak of prophetic ministry in the church, we're really talking about all the revelatory gifts, which include the Word of Wisdom, Word of Knowledge, and prophecy proper. In addition, we could include visions and dreams in this general family.

- **Word of Knowledge** – A specific piece of information about someone that you could not have known in the natural: "Your name is John."
- **Word of Wisdom** – Spiritual insight into a specific situation, giving guidance on the proper way to handle it: "You need to reduce the price on your house by $20,000 in order to sell it."
- **Prophecy** – Predictive information about future situations: "You're going to get an opportunity to switch careers in the next month."

- **Dreams and Visions**—Extended images or visual scenarios played out. Dreams usually refer to things we see when we're sleeping, and visions occur while awake.

We should not get too caught up in the distinctions between these gifts. In ministry situations they often blend together. The value in listing them is to help us understand and develop different capacities in revelation.

Parts of Prophecy

Prophecy has three parts: Revelation, Interpretation, and Application. We can see this in the story of Pharaoh's dream, during Joseph's life. (Genesis 41:17-36).

So Pharaoh spoke to Joseph, In my dream, behold, I was standing on the bank of the Nile; and behold, seven cows, fat and sleek came up out of the Nile, and they grazed in the marsh grass. Lo, seven other cows came up after them, poor and very ugly and gaunt, such as I had never seen for ugliness in all the land of Egypt; and the lean and ugly cows ate up the first seven fat cows. Yet when they had devoured them, it could not be detected that they had devoured them, for they were just as ugly as before. Then I awoke. I saw also in my dream, and behold, seven ears, full and good, came up on a single stalk; and lo, seven ears, withered, thin, and scorched by the east wind, sprouted up after them; and the thin ears swallowed the seven good ears. Then I told it to the magicians, but there was no one who could explain it to me. (Revelation)

Now Joseph said to Pharaoh, Pharaoh's dreams are one and the same; God has told to Pharaoh what He is about to do. The seven good cows are seven years; and the seven good ears are seven years; the dreams are one and the same. The seven lean and ugly cows that came up after them are seven years, and the seven thin ears scorched by the east wind will be seven years of famine. It is as I have spoken to Pharaoh: God has shown to Pharaoh what He is about to do. Behold, seven years of great abundance are coming in all the land of Egypt; and after them seven years of famine will come, and all the abundance will be forgotten in the land of Egypt, and the famine will ravage the land. So the abundance will be unknown in the land because of that subsequent famine; for it will be very severe. Now as for the repeating of the dream to Pharaoh twice, it means that the matter is determined by God, and God will quickly bring it about. (Interpretation)

Now let Pharaoh look for a man discerning and wise, and set him over the land of Egypt. Let Pharaoh take action to appoint overseers in charge of the land, and let him exact a fifth of the produce of the land of Egypt in the seven years of abundance. Then let them gather all the food of these good years that are coming, and store up the grain for food in the cities under Pharaoh's authority, and let them guard it. Let the food become as a reserve for the land for the seven years of famine which will occur in the land of Egypt, so that the land will not perish during the famine. ***(Application)***

- **Revelation** is when God reveals something. This may be symbolic or cryptic. Pharaoh had a dream of 7 fat cows and 7 lean cows.
- **Interpretation** is making sense of what you saw. Joseph had to decode Pharaoh's vision in order to know it meant famine was coming.
- **Application.** Knowing what a revelation means is not the same as knowing what to do about it. After interpreting Pharaoh's dream, Joseph then had to tell him what to do to save Egypt from famine.

Being mature in prophetic ministry means developing skill in each of these three areas. Each part has some natural knowledge combined with the inspiration of the Holy Spirit. It made sense that God would use a one thin cow to symbolize one year of famine, but Joseph relied on the Holy Spirit to interpret and give wisdom for this situation. We don't just throw Revelation at people, we pray for and practice interpretation and application.

What You Believe Matters

Prophecy must move through two human vessels before it reaches a person's heart: you and the person. Because of this, even if you have good revelation from God, your interpretation or application can be thrown off by what you believe. This is why it is important for us to develop godly perspectives about life. Then, when we give a word, we will be able to apply it correctly.

Exercising Discernment

"Sir, I perceive you are a prophet..." – John 4:19

When Jesus spoke with the woman at the well, He spoke in such an understated way that she perceived He was speaking prophetically to her only midway through their conversation. He did not prophesy in any kind of way that would draw attention to Himself, or reveal that He was actually God. He modeled a naturally supernatural approach in an everyday kind of ministry situation we ourselves could face.

If God on earth ministered in such low-key ways, we can take the pressure off ourselves to perform mighty feats for those we pray for. You don't have to impress anyone with your level of revelation. Sometimes you may get a lot of revelation but the person only needs a tiny piece in order to have the heart revelation God wants them to have. Or you may get just a small thing which you think is completely insignificant but opens up a large amount of revelation or healing for someone. The important thing is to ask and obey God in the process.

Jesus asked him [the blind man], "What do you want me to do for you?"
–Mark 10:51

It may have been obvious what the blind beggar needed, but Jesus still asked. He asked not because He didn't know, but because He was gracious and wanted to see the man to express his own faith. Nor was He directive. We are not directive with our prophecies. A person's decisions must always remain their own. If you have something serious to say or advise, take the conversation offline and have a normal discussion as friends. You can also ask questions during prayer ministry to prevent awkward situations—"Do you have any children, Bob?" At all times, the person's security and dignity are paramount, not our status as prophetic ministers. We "cover" people as we pray.

GETTING REVELATION

Getting revelation for someone else in prophetic ministry is similar to hearing God's voice for yourself. You believe He wants to speak and will speak. God is a communicating God.

Starting the Car

Sometimes you may have a strong prophetic impression that jump starts your prayer over someone, but most of the time you will need to "start the car" before praying out loud. Get quiet and invite the Lord to speak. You may pray in tongues a little bit or just wait on the Lord. Sometimes simple, general prayer is a good way to get the engine going—thanking the Lord for the person and their life, for what He is doing. Then more revelation will flow.

> For in Christ Jesus neither circumcision nor uncircumcision counts for anything, but only **faith working through love**. – Galatians 5:6

The first and most important part of getting revelation is to love the person you're praying for. Another way of saying this is, if you want to grow in prophecy, you should seek to grow in love. As you connect to God's heart for a person, you will also connect to God's thoughts for them. When you begin to speak over someone, posture your heart in a place of love for their life, and their calling, and then begin to speak out of that place.

> "Someone deliberately touched me, for I felt the healing power go out from me..."
> – Luke 8:46

When we take a moment to connect to God in love for the person we're praying for, the presence of God may physically touch them—whether they are a believer or not. Many times, that touch from God is the main thing that they need.

Polishing the Glass

> For now we see through a glass dimly, but then face to face. Now I know in part; but then shall I know, even as also I am known.
> –1 Corinthians 13:12

We see through a glass dimly into the heavenly world. We can see more clearly as we are less tied to this world, and more tied to that one. Because love is the catalyst, it's important to maintain a lifestyle and builds and reinforces love.

> For prophecy never had its origin in the human will, but prophets, though human, spoke from God as they were carried along by the Holy Spirit.

Prophecy usually works by "jumping off the cliff." You begin to pray for someone and you get more revelation about them. Often as a group of people pray together, a "flow" of revelation will come forward about that person. Don't be afraid to wait or pause. The Holy Spirit is within you. Therefore, most of what He says will emerge from within you; do not look for fireworks.

Ways God Speaks

Once you've gotten the car started, it is time to start growing in your ability to prophesy. This can be done by realizing some of the different ways God speaks.

➤ **Ideas.** The most basic way for God to speak is through a fresh idea. God is percolating his thoughts through our thoughts. This can be as simple as thinking of someone you haven't thought about in a while.

➤ **Pictures.** You might see a picture of some kind. It does not have to be a super-clear and stunning picture, it may just be an "impression" or something crossing your imagination that was not there before.

➤ **Words.** Sometimes you will hear God speak like an inner voice. This can be simple, like a phrase popping into your mind, or it can be stronger where it feels like someone actually said something in your head. In rare cases, God's voice can be so audible that someone else hears it.

➤ **Feelings.** Feelings are a very common way for God to speak. When you begin to think of someone or you lay hands on them, your human capacity for empathy connects to their feelings even if they haven't told you anything about them. As you begin to describe and speak to those feelings, your words emerge as prophecy.

➤ **Circumstances.** While many circumstances are the result of logical things in our lives, there are those moments when you realize that what is going on is not accidental. God is speaking by bringing your attention to a certain situation, often to confirm something, provide direction, or give you insight.

Interacting with Revelation

Flowing in the prophetic is like following a thread. As you pull the thread, you see and hear more. You can interact with revelation by asking God questions. These questions are usually thoughts or intentions of the heart, not out-loud questions.

For example, if you get a sense that someone has children, you can ask God, "Is it a daughter or a son?" When you imagine a daughter, it may not "feel right" but when you imagine a son, it "feels better." This feeling associated with true revelation is the same feeling you feel during worship or any other encounter with God. It is a kind of barometer that helps you hone in or get more specific as you prophesy.

Getting details like names and phone numbers from God requires a high level of revelation, but by following this kind of "binary" logic where you put questions before the Lord that are true or false, you can expand the level of revelation you get. It also keeps you in relationship with God as you pray.

PRACTICAL TIPS

Here are some practical tips, we have learned from experience which will help you to be more effective.

Don't Stress

Some people who are against the working of the Holy Spirit try to demand 100% accuracy out of prophetic people. This is a misunderstanding of God's relationship to us in the New Testament era. In the OT, prophets were often the mouthpiece for an entire kingdom and public policy; one wrong word could lead a nation to military or spiritual disaster.

In the NT church, prophecy is given for the edification of believers and unbelievers (1 Cor. 14:24-25). The Holy Spirit lives inside of us and desires to speak through us. This is not an autonomic process. Whatever God says has to pass through us. Because of this, there is potential for error. We grow in faith, revelation, and accuracy through practice.

> *Do not treat prophecies with contempt, but test all things. Hold fast to what is good. –1 Thess. 5:20-21*

We are not under an old covenant mindset. Prophecy is a gift for the church and should be examined; anything not good can be let go.

Know your Limits

> *We have different gifts, according to the grace given to each of us. If your gift is prophesying, then prophesy in accordance with your faith.*
> *–Romans 12:6*

Prophecy is according to the grace we have been given and the faith we have. You should always stretch your faith from where you are, but recognize the measure you have been given. For example, if you have never gotten a word of knowledge at all, it might not be best to start by trying to get names and phone numbers.

People Are Different

You will find with enough practice that you can get a word for anyone at any time, but some people are easier than others to prophesy over:

- **Hungry:** Someone who is intensely seeking the Lord will almost "glow" in the Spirit. Revelation almost jumps off of a person like this and you may find you have a lot to say or that what you say seems "clearer."

- **Emotional:** People who are naturally very emotional and transparent are easier to prophesy over. Some are encouraging to the flesh because they seem to cry or resonate over every word you ever give them!
- **Struggling:** People going through a very hard season—severe sickness, depression/suicide, anxiety—are often easy to prophesy over. You may feel their pain immediately after laying hands on them or a sense of darkness.
- **Bound up:** People in extreme bondage often give off a feeling when you lay hands on them as well. Lust and anger are relatively common to feel.
- **Reserved:** People who are extremely reserved can be more challenging to prophesy over, because they themselves are not aware of their own emotional state. Sometimes people like this will act like you are not getting accurate revelation about them even when it's exactly correct.

Be Life-Giving

Prophecy is about edification, exhortation, and encouragement. People should feel clearer and built up after you have prophesied over them. They should feel motivated to think about or take their next step. Be positive when you pray, even if there is something serious or corrective in the revelation you have.

Be Discreet

Prophecy is not about booming someone's sins from the pulpit, or even quietly letting them know that *you know.* If God reveals someone's sin to you, ask Him how He wants you to pray. God often will break a person more through a loving and a discerning word, than through direct confrontation.

If God reveals something that might be embarrassing to the person you're praying for, also use discretion and ask God for a Scripture or way to communicate the freedom or positive thing He is moving forward.

In rare occasions, God will use you to give a firm, correcting word, but you should take this aside in a private, discussion-oriented conversation. God speaks prophetically through a "friend" role just as much as through a prayer ministry role. Use the Golden Rule here and be prepared to love and cover a person whose world has been exposed.

Share the Floor

In a ministry situation where there is more than one person praying, it is important to share the floor. Don't go too long or too in detail about any vision or impression you had. This can be hard to listen to and makes the ministry seem like it's about you. Ask God what He wants you to share, and take turns. You may find that going back and forth between you and your partner(s) creates an "magnification" effect where more revelation comes forth, enough to really break through to the person in need.

QUESTIONS

1. What practices do you use to help "jump start" the car, when needing to pray or prophesy over someone?
2. Why is it important to get in touch with God's love flow for someone, as you pray over them?
3. Which way(s) that God speaks feels the most natural/unnatural for you?

ACTIVATION

Prophetic Prayer. Get into groups smaller than six people, and practice getting revelation for each other. Put one person in the middle, invite the Holy Spirit to speak to you all as a group, then ask God to give you his heart for that person. The person receiving prayer should not give any information about their life or situation to start. Those praying should try to get not just revelation, but also interpretation and application. If you get revelation but cannot interpret or apply it, ask the group to see if someone else can help. Practice giving what you got, but try not to dominate the time. Share the floor, and be life-giving in your interpretation.

At the end, the person in the middle should give feedback to the group. Have them highlight any words that really spoke to them or were a match for their situation. Those who prayed may share about how they received their revelations. Repeat for as many people as there is time.

STEPS YOU COULD TAKE

1. Practice praying prophetically with someone who has a different style than you— someone who gets ideas, feelings, pictures, etc. Ask them what they do, and try that to see if it works for you too.
2. Practice laying hands on someone and getting the love flow for them for at least one minute before praying for them. Then practice getting the love flow before even laying hands on them. Ask them to give you feedback about what they felt.
3. Practice praying prophetically over several of your "safe" friends this week. Get a sense of how people feel differently to pray over. Don't forget to ask God for revelation and interpretation before praying, and write down any good "hits" you make.

THE PROPHETIC FRAME OF REFERENCE

SEASONS OF LIFE

God works with people throughout the course of their life, trying to draw them deeper with him. As prophetic ministers, we join God in this process. We seek to discern where people are in their lives, and connect them to what God would say about that phase. There are several key principles for doing this.

Understanding Time and Seasons

A person's life will naturally break up into logical timeframes, with significant points of reference.

> And he made of one every nation of men to dwell on all the face of the earth, having determined their appointed **seasons**, and the bounds of their habitation. — Acts 17:26

> And God said, Let there be lights in the firmament of the heaven to divide the day from the night; and let them be for signs, and for **seasons**, and for days, and years. — Genesis 1:14

Every person's life proceeds through different "seasons." There are the basic phases of life pertaining to age—students, young married couples, older adults, etc.—but there are also spiritual seasons pertaining to spiritual growth. When we speak prophetically, it is helpful to understand that these seasons exist, as well as to speak to them.

A spiritual season can be as long or as short as the person walking through it chooses it to be, because the primary factor which determines the season of our life in God is our own growth. If we embrace the work of God in a season, it will go quickly, and if we do not embrace the work of God, it will repeat.

Boundaries of a Season

Major external factors, some of which are self-chosen, and some of which are not, are the key boundary points for a season. Addressing them often propels a person forwards. Before praying for someone, we consider:

> ➤ **Family**— Your family, past, present and future is a major part of your life. If something in your family life hurt you in the past, or is holding you back now, it affects everything else. Consider especially someone's parents, siblings, children, and spouse.
> ➤ **Friends** – Relationships with close friends define where we are in life. God may want to address how to leave, change, or add a relationship as part of positioning someone.

- ➤ **Employment–**Your job represents an important part of your "Kingdom assignment" and can be a severe drain or a major source of joy.
- ➤ **Church/Ministry Context–** Who we flow with is who we grow with (or not). A person's church situation or position within God's family is a powerful shaping influence and determines many things, including how they see themselves, and how they think others/God sees them.
- ➤ **Health–** Health issues can severely hinder someone's faith and calling. Ask God to reveal and heal, if they are willing. Sometimes a prophetic revelation can release the faith for healing.

Sometimes as prophetic people we assume a random starting point for getting revelation, as though a person has no touchpoints. But when you minister to someone, consider each of these factors. You can use these life-defining variables as touchpoints, offer them up to God, and ask Him for revelation. Ask to Him to speak to any constraints of this season to help the new one begin.

THE PROMOTION PROCESS

As we walk with God here on earth, we are given the opportunity to grow in our capacity for God. This happens through a promotion process.

Testing or Promotion?

> *"Simon, Simon, Satan has asked to sift all of you as wheat. But I have prayed for you, Simon, that your faith may not fail. And when you have turned back, strengthen your brothers." – Luke 22:31-32*

Peter was growing in his capacity in ministry, had been to the mountain with Jesus, had gotten revelation of Jesus' identity, walked on water, and was tapped to lead the team after Jesus died. But before Peter could be promoted, Satan had the opportunity to stop him. Jesus interceded for Peter so he could pass that test and be promoted to what God had in store for him, to build the church.

> *The devil took Him [Jesus] to the holy city and set him down on the pinnacle of the Temple, and said, "If you are the Son of God, throw yourself down..."*

> *Again, the devil took Him to a very high mountain and showed Him the kingdoms of the world and all their glory. "All this I will give you," he said, "if you bow down and worship me..." –Matthew 4:6-9*

Jesus was similarly tested by Satan over the exact Word for His life. The enemy designs customized traps to keep people from believing or walking in their callings. Through the Holy Spirit, however, every trap is an opportunity to confront the devil behind it and defeat him.

> *When tempted, no one should say, "God is tempting me." For God cannot be tempted by evil, nor does he tempt anyone. – James 1:13*

From God's angle, you're facing promotion, but from Satan's angle, you're facing a test. God cheers you on and shows you how to win, while the devil tries to defeat you and makes you feel like you've lost.

Talking about God "testing" someone tends to give the wrong impression of God's role in this process. It is common in prophetic circles to use this language, but it can distance the person you're praying for from God or even extend their pain. If they think their circumstances are ordained, they will not confront them with the force necessary to defeat the trap.

All of us who pursue God have times like this, even if we aren't aware of them. The process of God promoting you involves conquering your personal weaknesses and maturing in capabilities you have not fully developed. Most people need a coach out of their bad seasons, not just a mouthpiece. They need to feel God is on their side, not against them.

If God is for us, who can be against us? —Romans 8:31

Don't Extend the Wilderness!

A time of promotion and testing usually happens in a "wilderness." These are difficult seasons or moments in a person's life. Times of adversity are not pre-ordained windows of suffering, but times of opposition for us to overcome. It is important that we do not prophesy people into the wilderness or encourage them to stay there, but that we help them out of the wilderness.

It takes eleven days to go from Horeb to Kadesh Barnea by the Mount Seir road . —Deuteronomy 1:2

God wanted to lead the Israelites out of the wilderness from Sinai (Horeb) in eleven days. Instead, because of their disobedience, it took them 40 years! We're not supposed to live in the desert. God wants to lead us to victory by taking us through the wilderness, not wandering around in it.

"And be sure of this: I am with you always, even to the end of the age." —Matthew 28:20

In our difficult seasons of life, Jesus walks alongside us. Even when we wander or stray, and cause ourselves pain, Jesus takes the pain and walks with us. When you pray for someone in a wilderness season, you are like an Emmaus prophet on the road alongside others, as Jesus was. Minister comfort and optimism, and where Jesus is in the midst of whatever is going on.

No weapon formed against you shall prosper. —Isaiah 54:17

On a practical note, if someone is repeatedly coming to you for prayer for the same situation, they are likely in a wilderness season. It may be from the enemy or their own design, but they need encouragement. Praying general comfort from the Psalms or Scriptures is good in these circumstances because, as David's life shows, some trials are long and hard to defeat. Wait for the Lord to tell you if/when to prod someone out of their wilderness, and do not pressure a person to make choices or specific decisions. The main thing is that they feel like God has designed their pathway out, not their pathway in, and is for them.

UNHELPFUL BOXES

We have to be careful not to let our preconceived notions limit what we say. God is very "out of the box" in terms of what he can do with someone's life. If you allow him to lead you, you can actually learn things you didn't know about God while you are prophesying!

End Times Madness

> In these last days he has spoken to us by his Son, whom he appointed heir of all things, and through whom also he made the universe.
> – Hebrews 1:2

Study of the End Times is often referred to as "prophecy," yet it is an area of theology which can especially distort prophetic ministry. The sense that the world is going to end at any moment has a way of distorting what you would say prophetically by altering what you prophesy to be:

- **Overly Urgent.** "And if Jesus tarries tonight..." or "In these Last Days..." This can create an unusually high sense of urgency, bordering on panic.
- **Overly Hyped.** It can create an over-hyped interpretation of what God is doing. "You are being called as prophet for the Last Days... " is a way of attaching a very heady significance to what God is doing.
- **Convey a Limited Viewpoint.** Focusing on the sudden return of Christ blocks you from seeing the large panorama of what God wants to do through someone's life, and in the world at large over the course of decades.

Ultimately, End Times theology is not a pillar of truth for ministry. Although some portion of prophecy does deal with future and End Times events, the prophecy we are all instructed to pursue in 1 Corinthians 12-14 is for the edification of the church. This kind of prophecy unlocks people because they experience the reality of God seeing them, knowing them, caring for them, and supporting their godly desires. The End Times element does not tend to build people up because people need to come into contact with the beauty of their future, not an apocalyptic vision.

A Too-Small Kingdom

Many of us have been trained to think of Christianity as something that only happens inside of a church or only pertains to ministry activities. This is does not properly account for the breadth of God's work in people's lives.

> Then at Belshazzar's command, Daniel was clothed in purple, a gold chain was placed around his neck, and he was proclaimed the third highest ruler in the kingdom. – Daniel 5:29

He made a highly consecrated man, Daniel, the ruler of an incredibly pagan nation, Babylon. In the same way, God can use a very wide variety of callings and pursuits to advance His Kingdom.

When you speak over someone, think bigger than traditional ministry boxes. Don't assume that God cannot use a pursuit that may seem worldly on its surface to glorify him. There are Models for Christ, Athletes in Action, and Hollywood film directors and politicians who have consecrated themselves to the Lord. God can use our earthly pursuits to advance the Kingdom if we submit them to Him.

Hyper-Immediacy

> *Therefore we do not become discouraged [utterly spiritless, exhausted, and*
> *wearied out through fear]. Though our outer man is [progressively]*
> *decaying and wasting away, yet our inner self is being [progressively] renewed*
> *day after day. – 2 Corinthians 4:16, Amplified*

Although God can do a great deal in a single encounter, our life is comprised of what happens day after day. He does most things through gradual processes or progressive unfolding.

> *Do not be conformed by the pattern of this world but be transformed by the*
> *renewing of your mind –Romans 12:2*

The process of renewal only begins at salvation. We embark on a journey towards becoming like Christ, and to do that we must be reshaped. At first we were "conformed" to the world's ways, or slowly shaped by repeated exposure. God then asks us to be transformed (slowly changed) into the image of Christ. The way we do that is by "renewing" our mind which implies a progressive, cleansing, substitutionary process.

Immature people expect an amazing thing to happen overnight instead of as a part of a process. This can creep into the way we prophesy. Apply the revelations you get to timelines that make sense in terms of how life actually works.

Appearance of Suddenness. Sometimes God does something which appears to be sudden, but which is really the result of a long term process. For example, someone is in a difficult financial situation, and they suddenly are given an amazing job opportunity. Because they were seeking the Lord and developing themselves in the midst of their difficulty, moving them to a new situation created a sudden shift, but it was actually long in the making.

As prophetic ministers, having realistic timelines is important because unrealistic ones can set people up for discouragement or disbelief. Grudges or heartsickness occurs with the expectations of immediacy. We embrace God's miraculous intervention but do not promote it above everyday life processes and decisions. God uses both.

> And I am sure of this, that he who **began** a good work in you will bring it to **completion** at the day of Jesus Christ. —Philippians 1:6

Much of Scripture exists to encourage the saints along their faithful journey to the end of their lives, even to the End of time. God asks us, as ministers, to stand with people in that journey. Our faith is something we've been given, to give. We pray things that we see, like "I believe God will give you…" but try not to build up expectations and timeframes that would discourage the person who actually has to walk out that journey.

"I See and Know All"

> For we know in part and we prophesy in part. —1 Corinthians 13:9

Although words of knowledge can be powerful, they do not entitle us to assume we know all or have all the answers. Usually we have just a part of the picture.

> The one who thinks he knows something does not yet know as he ought to know. —1 Corinthians 8:2

Even people seeking our prayers may not have the capacity to experience what we're assuming they need—whether salvation, baptism in the Holy Spirit, or other help. They may not see themselves the way we do or connect to the message given, even if we're seeing correctly. We do not force change or take that responsibility upon us, even for a friend or someone hurting deeply.

> "You do not know what you are asking…To sit at my right or my left is not for me to grant." —Mark 10:38-40

Jesus had a very delicate balance of being direct but not taking over the discipleship process. He encouraged people to dig within themselves. While a little "course correction" may be exactly what God is trying to give someone, we do not insert ourselves into God's place. We simply give them a peek at what we're seeing, and allow the Holy Spirit to enlarge that in their hearts if we are correct.

QUESTIONS

1. Do you have any theologies that would promote wilderness seasons, a hyper sense of urgency, or the God-is-testing-you perspective on those you pray for?
2. How can you adjust your own language to fit more normal expectations and timeframes in someone's life?
3. Consider some of the major seasons you have walked through in your life so far. Can you identify major issues with family, friends, job, ministry, or health that propelled you in or out of those seasons?

ACTIVATION

Prophetic Key Events. Divide into small groups. Try to mix it up from the last time. Put one person in the middle to practice getting revelation for them. Start with someone who hasn't had lots of prayer yet. Instead of asking God for insight into the person specifically, ask about each of the key areas of life:

- Family
- Friends
- Job
- Church/Ministry
- Health

Debrief by talking to each other about how you received each revelation that was shared. Repeat for as many people as there is time. Remember to be positive and share the floor.

STEPS YOU CAN TAKE

1. Listen to several prophets online and note any exaggeration of time or level of impact—phrases like "worldwide," "suddenly," "End Times" or "Last Days," and "to the nations," etc. Consider how this affects both the person being prayed for and the audience who witnesses the prophecy.
2. Have a conversation with someone dealing with significant issues in one of the above categories (family, friends, job, church/ministry, health). To get a better sense of what feelings or thoughts are common to that season, take notes on anything that sounds applicable to another person dealing with that same area—for example, "I'm so unfulfilled at my job" or "I'm afraid he might be really sick."

PROPHETIC PITFALLS

COMMON MISTAKES

In prayer ministry, and prophetic ministry especially, there are common pitfalls many of us encounter. Some of them are things that stem from pride in our own hearts, others come from the person we're praying for or the overall culture we're ministering in.

Idols Must Be Torn Down

> They say to the seers, "See no more visions!" and to the prophets, "Give us no more visions of what is right! Tell us pleasant things, prophesy illusions. – Isaiah 30:10

> But Jehoshaphat asked, "Is there no longer a prophet of the Lord here whom we can inquire of?" The king of Israel answered Jehoshaphat, "There is still one prophet through whom we can inquire of the Lord, but I hate him because he never prophesies anything good about me, but always bad. He is Micaiah son of Imlah." –1 Kings 22:7-8

We all have the potential to have an idol in our hearts. Sometimes even a committed Christian can allow an idol to build up, usually around their personal goals and dreams. Their desire to serve God gets mixed with other desires, or they are not in a good relationship posture, and then they develop their own agenda that is not the Lord's. An idol is ultimately a spiritual reality, and so it can lead an inexperienced or less than courageous prophetic person to prophesy "smooth things" or things the person wants to hear, rather than what God sees.

One way to deal with an idol is to speak to the things which drive the person's connection to it, and a new pathway that God wants in order to build a stronger connection to them.

Prophetic Inflation

> We have different gifts according to the grace given us. If someone's gift is prophecy, let him use it **in proportion** to his faith; if it is serving, let him serve; if it is teaching, let him teach... –Romans 12:6-7

One of the ways that prophets miss is by inflating a revelation they get. It is easy to get excited or to want something to seem bigger and more important than it is, especially if the person you are praying for is a friend, a person with influence, or a person who has lost hope. This can lead you to take a true revelation and stretch it to the point where it could have the opposite effect.

Example: You're praying for someone and you see a picture of them evangelizing. The correct thing to do is consider the measure they have been given, and speak a logical step of growth to that, i.e. "God wants to use you more in evangelism." However, what some prophetic people will do is inflate the scope: "God is going to make you a great evangelist!" Now you have set the person up for disappointment. Instead of them feeling encouraged to do more evangelism, now they are hoping for the big break that will make them Reinhard Bonnke. When it doesn't come, they will be disappointed.

Inflation like this can be twofold: If you hype what God said, they might then hype what you said on top of that, and expect something way beyond what God was speaking. They could end up disappointed with you, with the prophetic, and even with God.

> *For by the grace given me I say to every one of you: Do not think of yourself more highly than you ought, but think of yourself with sober judgment, according to the measure of faith God has given you.*
> *–Romans 12:3*

The God–Card

As we mentioned in an earlier session, we want to avoid dramatizing our ministry with phrases like, "Thus saith the Lord," or "God told me..." which is also a kind of prophetic inflation. Neither Paul nor the disciples spoke that way even though they had the authority to author the Words of God for eternity! When Jesus spoke, He put responsibility on Himself—"the words *I* tell you..." "Truly, truly *I* say to you..." He did not dramatize His presentation, i.e. "The Father tells you..." or "The God of the Universe says..." even though He could have.

Overdramatizing the Lord's agency in our lives as we pray over others has a tendency to remove the person's natural sense of agency in their own life.

Doom and Gloom

The other side of inflation is doom and gloom. Some prophetic people, inspired by the Old Testament, prefer to give a lot of warnings and correction in their ministry. The main problem with doing this is not that God never has a warning or word of correction, but that they easily put people into fear or bitterness.

Example: A minister prophesies that you will soon go through a "tornado" in your life, a "tumultuous season where God is going to turn things upside down to draw you closer to him." This will put you on eggshells and make you question whether everything you're doing is going to blow up in your face—or worse, whether God is against you, is going to take your prosperity or health away, etc. It paints the wrong picture of God. If you do get a word of warning or correction, find a way to pray into the right things that would spare the person any pain, or talk to the person about the issue in conversation outside the context of prayer and ministry.

Fear is a stronger emotion than hope so it can produce quick results, but hope produces rich, long-term results. Faith, hope, and love all take a lifetime to build so we must be careful not to shatter that with our words.

TRICKY AREAS

These are areas which are sensitive in prayer so we use special care when dealing with them. The Golden Rule is a really good guide for how to handle most prayer situations. We avoid exaggeration, condemnation, manipulation, because we would want the same from others. We also guard our own hearts.

Avoiding Embarrassment

> *"If your brother or sister sins, go and point out their fault, just between the two of you. If they listen to you, you have won them over."*
> *–Matthew 18:15*

Sometimes God may show you something that would be embarrassing in public. This could be because it's a sin issue, or because it's particularly personal in nature, or because of what others might perceive if they heard it. For example, if someone is in an unhealthy relationship and the other person is present with them, you should use discretion and try to take the first aside. Ask a question that will keep the pressure low and give them the opportunity to reveal the situation and own what they ask for.

This is especially important when praying for leaders in the church in public, such as pastors, small group leaders, or worship team members. Be mindful of what others will hear and how they may hear it. We always want to show honor and discretion. Prayer is very personal and private by its very nature.

Mates & Dates

We don't prophesy specific mates into someone else's life. This is for several reasons:
- **Your Own Emotions.** Your own interests and emotions in a dating/marital situation can get inserted even if you don't know it. For example, if you really want a certain friend to get married, this can taint your revelation or interpretation.
- **Their Emotions.** Your friend's attraction toward a certain person, or strong desire for a mate in general has a high potential to cloud your vision. You can end up speaking to what they want instead of what God is saying.
- **Trumping their will.** Marriage is the biggest decision of a person's life. God will lead us, but he always wants us to make the choice. Speaking for God on this topic can have very serious consequences if you are wrong. On the other hand, if you are right, you can trump someone's will and create a situation where they resent God during the difficult times of a marriage they would have chosen for themselves anyway!

In summary, in the context of prayer and prophetic ministry, we aren't matchmakers. If you feel strongly led about the health (or ill health) of a current relationship, take it into a natural discussion and ask questions without drawing conclusions about future decisions about that relationship.

Babies

Babies are an area where we also need to exercise special care. Babies are a highly emotional part of a woman's life and a very intimate decision for a couple. A prophecy or word of knowledge about children can have the effect of pushing someone to do something they wouldn't have otherwise done. Or you may mistake what God *wants* to do for what he actually is doing. Therefore we do not prophesy babies or numbers of children into someone's life. If you feel strongly led, ask them about it, and then pray in agreement.

INTEGRITY ISSUES

Integrity issues are more serious than mistakes. We need to work hard to preserve our integrity. Speaking on behalf of the Lord is a very serious responsibility, and those who do so for selfish gain will be judged strictly.

> *As God's steward, an overseer **must be above reproach**—not self-absorbed, not quick tempered, not given to drunkenness, not violent, not greedy for money. Instead, he must be hospitable, a lover of good, self-controlled, upright, holy, and disciplined. He must hold firmly to the trustworthy message as it was taught, so that by sound teaching he will be able to encourage others and refute those who contradict this message. —Titus 1:7-9*

Being a prayer minister is being God's steward—not of church operations, but of people's hearts. Praying for others is an honor and privilege at the church and before the Lord. We want to steward His will with reverence for Him and for the loving care of others.

Keep Your Heart Pure

As prayer ministers, we must be accountable for anything in our own hearts that would push us in the wrong direction. Whatever is inside of you will flow into others. We never prophesy out of a position of pride or judgment, as this can seriously damage someone. We prophesy only out of love and encouragement. If we are unable to do that, we aren't ready to prophesy.

Passing off Natural Knowledge as Prophecy

God can give us revelation about things we know in the natural, or use what we know as a starting point for revelation, which is perfectly legitimate. However, we should never pass off something that we know in the natural as a prophetic revelation. That's fraud.

Example: If you know from Facebook that someone's birthday is coming up, you can't say, "God showed me your birthday is coming up." But you could say, "I know your birthday is coming up. God really wants to celebrate you on your birthday."

Manipulation

Prophetic manipulation occurs when you insert what you want to happen into the middle of what God wants to say, or even worse, when you pass off what you want as what God wants. The prophetic gift is not given for your benefit, it is given for the benefit of the person and for others. To be "above reproach," you have to take special steps to separate yourself from any situation that could create a conflict of interest.

Example: You are a leader in the church and want your own church to grow, and you think this person would add a lot to the church. You know they need a church home, so you prophesy, "God wants to plant you here at this Church." There are numerous problems with this:

- **Natural Knowledge.** If you know all of this in the natural, it's not prophetic.
- **Over-specificity/Control.** Being so specific prevents them from having any real choice, which will undermine their relationship with the church and God even if you are correct.
- **Self-Benefit.** You stand to benefit from their choice so it's an abuse of the gift, even if it's correct.
- **Conflation of Authority.** In general, you should not prophesy direction over someone you have spiritual authority over, because anything you say sounds coercive. Your will becomes mixed with God's will.

In summary, the principle is to always divest your own self-interest before sharing God's heart with someone. As long as you are out of the way, God can communicate His way.

Bringing People Back to the Source

> *"His sheep follow him because they know his voice. A stranger they will not follow, but will flee from him because for they do not know the voice strangers."*
> *–John 10:4-5*

Jesus promises His people that they can hear Him, which is the ultimate purpose of the Christian life. Growing in the prophetic can sometimes cause us to lose sight of that. As we practice hearing God better, and pray for more people who may not hear as well, there is the possibility of inadvertently cutting God out of the equation for them.

> *"For the testimony of Jesus is the spirit of prophecy" – Revelation 19:10*

If you feel pressure for a prophecy, direct them back to the source. One of the healthiest prayers you can pray for anyone is simply, "Let's just pray for God to speak to you this week about (X)." Or, "Let's ask God what He wants you to do." This keeps the focus on Jesus, both for them and for you.

QUESTIONS

1. Have you ever experienced being asked to pray for someone's idol, or something you felt was their own agenda rather than God's? How did you handle it?
2. Have you had the experience of being burned by a prophetic word? For example, by receiving an inflated word that was out of proportion to your position, by receiving a coercive word, or by receiving a cursing word that put fear into your heart?

ACTIVATION

Storytime. Get into groups of 3 or 4 and exchange stories. Ask: Have you ever made a mistake when praying for someone? How did you handle it, or how should you have handled it? Or, on the other hand, have you ever handled a challenging situation in a way that really worked well?

STEPS YOU CAN TAKE

1. Get before God and ask him to reveal if there's anything in your prophetic style that he wants you to correct. Don't feel condemned—we all make mistakes. Just repent and ask him to increase your sensitivity and wisdom on how to handle the people you pray for.
2. Start to keep a record of what you pray and prophesy over people in your circle, so that you can both be accountable for what you say as well as pray more into any challenging situations God may reveal to you.

USING SCRIPTURE IN PRAYER:

SYMBOLS

PROPHETIC INTERPRETATION OF SCRIPTURE

When you pray over someone, you can apply Scripture to contemporary situations, through the leading of the Holy Spirit. You can ask the Holy Spirit to give you Scriptural stories or analogies that will open up what God is doing in their life.

> *For these are not drunken, as you suppose, seeing it is but the third hour of the day. But **this is that** which was spoken by the prophet Joel.*
> *—Acts 2:15-16*

When tongues fell on the believers in Jerusalem, Peter got a word of wisdom through the Holy Spirit and knew which Scripture applied to the situation. He used the "this is that" principle to explain what was going on, based on the principle that "*that* which the Old Testament prophesies is fulfilled in *this* way in the New Testament." One famous Bible teacher says it this way, "The Old Testament is the New Testament concealed, and the New Testament is the Old Testament revealed."

We can use this principle in ministry settings. When we encounter situations or get revelation about someone's life, we should ask God, "Where is that in the Bible? Where can I find the analogy or wisdom that applies to what you have shown me?" The Holy Spirit can lead us to a passage and connect us to the meaning which matters most at that time.

Why it Matters

The Bible is the common language of Christians. We recognize its authority and are familiar with the stories. When you give someone a prophetic interpretation of their situation, using Scripture, you allow a person to write themselves into a Bible story and give them a "roadmap" for their own life experience. It legitimizes their experience, helps them see more clearly what is going on, helps them pull more revelation out of the Bible story you used. It becomes a "personal parable" to unlock what's going on.

Role of the Holy Spirit

> *The Spirit told Philip, "Go to that chariot and stay near it." Then Philip ran up to the chariot and heard the man reading Isaiah the prophet. "Do you understand what you are reading?" Philip asked. "How can I," he said, "unless someone explains it to me?" So he invited Philip to come up and sit with him. —Acts 8:29-31*

The Ethiopian eunuch, a highly educated royal official, did not understand what he was reading because he did not have someone to explain it to him. Philip, who was walking closely with the Holy Spirit, however, did understand and was able to explain it to him. The Holy Spirit is the key to proper interpretation and application of the Scripture.

In our regular devotions, we have the habit of reading random passages in the Bible and trying to squeeze meaning out of them for our lives, when the Holy Spirit can lead us to do the opposite: bring us to those Scriptures which apply to us and give insight to what is happening in our lives. He can do the same things for us as we pray prophetically over people.

ESCAPE THE BOX

In order to function in prophetic interpretation of Scripture during prayer, we have to break some preconceived molds about Bible interpretation.

The Box We're Trapped In

The contemporary method of Scriptural interpretation taught in seminaries can be extremely literal. This method is sometimes summed up by the popular saying below:

> "When the plain sense of Scripture makes common sense, seek no other sense."

The problem with this method is that it creates a box from which we cannot easily apply Scripture to our own lives. We read a story and think that the only point of the story is to learn about the character. Or we see a symbol and instead of interpreting that symbol, we assume its only relevance is its face value meaning. In other words, we lose a great deal of the genius and richness of Scripture.

While this method is popular, the "hyper-literal" approach cannot be correct because it does not match the method used by the apostles to interpret the Old Testament. In fact, very few Old Testament citations in the New Testament follow a literal "in context" reading. Let's look at one example:

> "Rise, take the child and his mother, and flee to Egypt, and remain there until I tell you... This was to fulfill what the Lord had spoken by the prophet, "Out of Egypt I called my son." –Matthew 2:15

Here, Matthew is quoting Hosea. But in context, at the time he wrote it, Hosea does not appear to be referring to the Messiah or any future event at all. He is referring to the history of Israel.

> When Israel was a child, I loved him, and out of Egypt I called my son.
> –Hosea 11:1

By modern interpretive standards, Matthew would be guilty of "taking the Scripture out of context." If you study OT quotations used by the apostles, most of them follow this pattern. The question then becomes, what method are the *writers* of Scripture using to interpret Scripture? They relied on symbols, typology, and the inspiration of the Holy Spirit.

Allegory vs. Typology

Symbols are things that stand for something else, such as a tree, a wall, a river. *Typology* is studying the growth of symbols within a text to see their larger story. When you begin to explore symbols and typology in the Bible, some educated scholars charge you with undermining the authority of the Scripture or "allegorizing the text," so let's clear up the difference:

Allegory uses a story in Scripture as a starting point to say something that has no direct correlation to the Scripture itself. (The Chronicles of Narnia is a contemporary allegory.) Each symbol in the story stands for something else, usually a bigger concept or truth that has to be "unlocked" by the reader and verified by the author. A true allegorical interpreter may even view the original Bible story as just a fable—something that did not happen, but contains a moral. Those who study typology, on the other hand, believe that:

1. The Scripture is a true account of real events.
2. The apostles used this method of Biblical interpretation so we should too.
3. Scripture tells us how to interpret itself and holds the keys to do so.
4. All good interpretation builds on a long chain of interpretation starting with Creation and growing through the Biblical text.

UNDERSTANDING SYMBOLS AND TYPES

Once we accept the validity of symbols and types we need to understand what they and how they function in the Bible. Then we can use them faithfully in prophecy or dream interpretation.

What is a Type?

A "type" is a special kind of symbol which foreshadows something in the future. Consider again, the Scripture used to explain the life of Jesus:

> When Israel was a child, I loved him, and out of Egypt I called my son.
> —Hosea 11:1

This Scripture works by making Israel a "type" of Jesus. It connects the story of Israel as a nation with the story of Jesus. You would then read Israel's story differently from plain history—you would read it as their being a disobedient type of Jesus, and Jesus as being a type of obedient Israel.

The type is not limited to the connection between Jesus and Israel however. It is a Scriptural trajectory which begins with Abraham's journey out of Egypt, and is replayed in the lives of his descendants including Jacob (Israel), his twelve sons, and then the nation as a whole. The larger principle at work is God getting his children out of "Egypt"—the worldly system that leads to death. Jesus fulfills this type, by delivering us from the world's curse of death, but then it becomes a spiritual pattern that applies to all of us now, because Jesus lives in us and continually calls out of the world as we walk with Him.

Types are symbols which represent patterns of God's activity and human interaction with it, through time. They begin in the Old Testament, are fulfilled in the New Testament, and then have their application in the church age, in New Testament life. When we connect someone today to one of these symbols or types, we are opening up a whole new layer of personalized meaning to them.

Symbols Begin During Creation

Contrary to the hyper-literal reading, understanding symbols must embrace the flexibility of interpretation. It is a process very similar to interpreting literature. However, good interpretations are always grounded in the real-life function of the symbol and in context (i.e. Egypt's ears of corn, cows).

Every Biblical symbol has its root in the created order. God is the Creator. Everything he created has a function and is different from other things based on that function. When you want to interpret a symbol, begin by asking yourself questions like:

- What does this thing do?
- How is it different from other similar things and how is it the same?

Starting with Creation, the Bible then builds interpretations for many things and categories of things which give us clues on how to interpret them.

How Symbols Function in the Bible: The Robe

Genesis is sometimes referred to as the "seed plot of the Bible" because most of the symbolic themes of the Bible appear there, even if they are only in tiny "seed" form. The way that a symbol functions in Genesis becomes a basis for how the symbol is used through the rest of Scripture. Consider clothing. The first appearance of clothing is in Genesis:

> Then the eyes of both of them were opened, and they realized they were naked; so they sewed fig leaves together and **made coverings** for themselves. – Genesis 3:7

> The LORD God made **garments** of skin for Adam and his wife and **clothed** them. –Genesis 3:21

In Genesis, the garment is a covering which represents the plan of salvation or spiritual authority. A manmade covering attempts to cover our shame, but God covers our guilt with his own divinely fashioned clothing.

> Now Israel loved Joseph more than any of his other sons, because he had been born to him in his old age; and he made an **ornate robe** for him... Then they got Joseph's robe, slaughtered a goat and dipped the robe in the blood. –Genesis 37:3,31

In the story of Joseph, the robe represents his father's favor on him, the Spiritual authority and gifting on his life.

> He put the tunic on Aaron, tied the sash around him, clothed him with the **robe** and put the ephod on him. He also fastened the ephod with a **decorative waistband**, which he tied around him. –Leviticus 8:7

The priests wear a special robe—a special covering—which follows the pattern of the Genesis story and represents God's plan of salvation.

> When I saw in the plunder a **beautiful robe** from Babylonia, two hundred shekels of silver and a bar of gold weighing fifty shekels, I coveted them and took them. They are hidden in the ground inside my tent, with the silver underneath. – Joshua 7:21

In the story of Aachan, he wanted to cover himself with the things of this world, his plan of salvation, the same way Adam and Eve had done.

> *See, my father, look at this piece of your **robe** in my hand! I cut off the corner of your **robe** but did not kill you. See that there is nothing in my hand to indicate that I am guilty of wrongdoing or rebellion.*
> *−1 Samuel 24:11*

In the story of Saul and David, David proves that he does not lust after Saul's authority by only cutting a small piece of his robe away—the rest of his spiritual authority is left intact.

> *So Elijah went from there and found Elisha son of Shaphat. He was plowing with twelve yoke of oxen, and was driving the twelfth pair. Elijah went up to him and threw his **cloak** around him. − 1 King 19:19*

Elijah threw his garment onto Elisha as a sign of bringing him under his spiritual authority and the intention to pass that authority to him.

> *They stripped him and put a **scarlet robe** on him. After they had mocked him, they took off the **robe** and put his own clothes on him. When they had crucified him, they divided up his **clothes** by casting lots. − Mathew 27:28,31,35*

In the story of Jesus, they mock his royal authority by putting a royal colored robe on him, and then stripped him of it and sold it, reminiscent of the way Joseph was stripped of his robe and therefore his dignity, authority, and covering. The robe here is scarlet, reflecting the blood of Christ, the source of our authority through Him and His plan of salvation.

> *"These in white **robes**—who are they, and where did they come from?"… "These are they who have come out of the great tribulation; they have washed their **robes** and made them white in the blood of the Lamb." − Revelation 7:13-14*

In the end, we are given robes which represent our faith in Jesus and cleansing by his blood. All the stains and sacrifices are gone, making them white.

EXAMPLE APPLICATION

Now that we understand what types and symbols are and how they function, we can look at an example of how to apply one.

Interpreting a Symbol: The Flower

Let's look at how we could interpret one very simple symbol: the flower.

> They spring up like **flower**s and wither away; like fleeting shadows, they do not endure. –Job 14:2

Here the flower represents something transient, which blooms for a moment but then disappears.

> **Flower**s appear on the earth; the season of singing has come, the cooing of doves is heard in our land. – Song of Solomon 2:12

Here the flower plays a more traditional role. It represents the coming excitement of spring – a new season of birth and growth.

> "And why do you worry about clothes? See how the **flower**s of the field grow. They do not labor or spin. – Matthew 6:28

In this Scripture, the flower is something beautiful which is cared for and cultivated by God, which Jesus connects to the way God cares for our lives.

In each of these interpretations, the author of Scripture is drawing on an aspect of the flower to illustrate a point by analogy. This is the same way God uses symbols in prophecy, in dreams or visions. Led by the Spirit, you can interpret the symbol based on the context of the person's life.

- If someone had a dream of flowers blooming and fading, it might represent something in the world which they are attracted to, but which is actually not to be pursued.
- If you got a picture of a flower in spring when praying for someone, it could refer to them beginning a new season when their beauty before the Lord will emerge.
- On the other hand, that same flower might represent God's special care for the person.

Common Bible interpreters would encourage a very narrow interpretation of a "flower," usually just a singular meaning. But in fact the Scripture itself opens up multiple interpretations—all which could be possible, any of which could have been intended by God. You would know which of these possible interpretations were correct based on the feelings given to you by the Holy Spirit when you picture the flower. He guides you to correct interpretations based within biblical guidelines.

We do this as led by the Holy Spirit. Even though a symbol generally follows a theme, there are always several possible interpretations and applications. As we bring the symbol before the Lord and consider its meaning and potential applications, we will usually feel more drawn to one over another. That is the one we should pray into.

Applying the Symbol

We apply symbols by identifying their function and then creating a point of correspondence to that person's life. Think of the symbol like a puzzle piece and the person's life like a puzzle. You have found the correct interpretation when the puzzle piece fits their life properly. We are doing what Peter did when he said, "This (situation in your life) is that (situation or symbol from the Bible)."

DREAM INTERPRETATION

Dreams usually contain many symbols. Not all dreams are from God. Some dreams are just a way our soul works through the various stresses of life. Other dreams are from the evil one to try and scare us. Ignore both of those kinds of dreams. When God speaks, the dream will often be especially vivid and insightful. These are the dreams we try to interpret.

Joseph's Dream

Pharaoh's dream that Joseph interpreted had symbols in it, which in retrospect make sense:

> (A) He was standing by the Nile, when out of the river there came up seven cows, sleek and fat, and they grazed among the reeds.
> (A') After them, seven other cows, ugly and gaunt, came up out of the Nile and stood beside those on the riverbank.
> (B) And the cows that were ugly and gaunt ate up the seven sleek, fat cows
>
> (A) Seven heads of grain, healthy and good, were growing on a single stalk.
> (A') After them, seven other heads of grain sprouted—thin and scorched by the east wind.
> (B) The thin heads of grain swallowed up the seven healthy, full heads
> — Genesis 41:1-7

The cows and ears of corn each stand for the function they perform in real life: a source of food and provision. The fact that the cows come up out of the Nile refers to the fact that Egypt depended on the flooding of the Nile for irrigation and farming. The fact that the one set ate the other refers to the coming years of difficulty which would consume all of the excess of the years of plenty.

Parallelism

Another interesting aspect of Pharaoh's dream is parallelism, which is used throughout the Bible. Parallelism uses comparing and contrasting to bring things into focus. In both dreams the same idea is repeated, first positive (A), then negative (A'), then there is a second idea (B). Joseph saw the parallelism and that helped him decode the dream. Instead of just looking at a cow, he could focus in on what is the *same* about a cow and corn. When two symbols that are similar appear, it helps bring focus.

QUESTIONS

1. How have you been taught to study the Scripture? What kind of results has that yielded in your personal studies?
2. Do you struggle with interpreting your own dreams or visions in prophecy? How can studying symbols or typology help you in interpreting and applying these images?

ACTIVATION

Dreams and Vision Interpretation. Divide into two or three smaller groups. First, if anyone has had a dream or vision that they cannot fully interpret, ask them to share it and then try to interpret it together. Be interactive if necessary and try to fit the clues into the puzzle of their life.

For the second phase, put someone on the middle and ask God to give a picture or image which connects to the life of that person. Instead of just giving an interpretation yourself, share the picture with others and explore interpretation options as a group. Finally, have the person in the middle try to interpret and apply it to themselves.

STEPS YOU CAN TAKE:

1. Use an online tool like BibleGateway to search the use and growth of a symbol like "temple" throughout the Bible. Make sure to include the Tabernacle, tents, or other forms of housing God's people used.
2. Do a small Bible study on how one NT author (i.e. Matthew, Luke, Paul) used Old Testament Scripture in their text. Look up a dozen or so original references to see the differences between the original context and the new context the NT author is applying it to.
3. Read a book or article by a popular typological interpreter of the Bible such as Greg Beale or Kevin Conner to see how they use Scripture to interpret Scripture—and get a LOT more out of the Bible than a simple devotional!

USING SCRIPTURE IN PRAYER: STORIES

UNDERSTANDING STORIES

Bible stories were not given to us just for fun and interest, but God has a purpose for them in our lives. Learning this purpose can make us effective in prayer.

What Stories are For

> These things **happened to them as examples** and were written down as warnings for us, on whom the culmination of the ages has come.
> −1 Corinthians 10:11

Paul explains to us one of the main interpretive keys for understanding the stories of the Old Testament. They were given to us as "examples." They are paradigms which correlate in various ways to our lives at different times.

> Elijah was a man **just like us.** He prayed earnestly that it would not rain, and it did not rain on the land for three and a half years. − James 5:17

The characters of the Old Testament did not go through situations that were unique to them. They were human and had to deal with the same types of issues that we do. We tend to think of the characters in the Bible like superheroes or fables instead of like real people with real emotions and struggles. Only when we understand that they went through all of the same kinds of human experiences that we do, can we connect our lives to theirs.

They Faced Choices

We have a tendency to read the Bible, and all history, as if it could only have happened the way that it did. In reality, all of the people in history have faced real choices just like we do, and then had to make those choices based on their limited knowledge and what was in them. Only once we see these choices can we connect their lives with our own.

> So Abram said to Lot, "Let's not have any quarreling between you and me, or between your herders and mine, for we are close relatives. Is not the whole land before you? Let's part company. **If you go to the left, I'll go to the right; if you go to the right, I'll go to the left."** Lot looked around and saw that the whole plain of the Jordan toward Zoar was well watered, like the garden of the Lord, like the land of Egypt. (This was before the Lord destroyed Sodom and Gomorrah.) **So Lot chose for himself the whole plain of the Jordan and set out toward the east**. The two men parted company. − Genesis 13:8-11

Abraham and Lot were having tensions and so Abraham gave his nephew a choice. Lot then had to make the decision. Most likely Abraham knew that Lot would choose the better land. However, if Lot had chosen differently, history and the subsequent chapters would have unfolded differently. In order to really identify with the actors, we have to consider what it was like to be Abraham/Lot in the moment, why he would have done what he did, and the fact that he could have done otherwise.

First the Natural, Then the Spiritual

However, that which is spiritual was not first, but that which is natural, and afterward that which is spiritual. – 1 Corinthians 15:46

The natural stories of the Old Testament are models of our spiritual lives in the New Testament. They experienced battles primarily in the natural realm, whereas we experience them primarily in the spiritual realm.

For our struggle is not against flesh and blood, but against the rulers, against the authorities, against the powers of this dark world and against the spiritual forces of evil in the heavenly realms. – Ephesians 6:12

Where the figures of the OT fought natural battles with natural enemies, we fight spiritual battles with spiritual enemies. Elements of a stories in the Old Testament really happened but usually take on a spiritual meaning in the New Testament. For example, David was an actual shepherd boy, but Jesus likens himself to "the Good Shepherd" from the line of David—a shepherd of people. Jesus gives a spiritual application to this natural activity which could be applied to other stories, such as Jacob and his sheep.

MAKE IT RELEVANT

Once we understand how stories function, we need to learn how to connect them to our own lives.

Translating the Story

Making Scripture come to life means translating the ancient realities into concepts that are contemporary and relevant to the person you are ministering to. While context changes greatly through the millennia, the basic realities of human existence are exactly the same (sin, love, hurt, hunger, family, adversity, etc.). We build analogies between the stories in the Bible and the story of our life based on these connection points. Part of this entails translating Biblical terms into terms we would use in our own lives.

Example: Adam and Eve stood naked in the garden and were tempted to eat a forbidden fruit by a talking snake. While this is not a situation that any of us will ever experience, we have similar experiences all the time when we are tempted by the enemy to do what is forbidden by God. In these cases, we can therefore see our situation through a biblical lens of choosing between "two trees in the garden."

Points of Connection

Our lives do not map exactly to Bible characters. However, every season of our life corresponds in some way to a moment encountered by a Bible character. We do not need to connect an entire story to a person we're praying for; we simply need to find a moment of connection and pray into that moment. As we see the connection, we pray into that particular point of correspondence and God will reveal and expand the connection to help them identify with the moment and the character in question. The moment may be a positive or a negative example, but if it is the latter, the Holy Spirit will make that known to them—for example, if they were Lot and tempted to choose the wrong path.

The Interpretive Gap

The authors of Scripture were selective in what details they used, depending on the message they were trying to emphasize to whom. We can see this in the gospels, where we have four different perspectives of the same events.

Similarly, they were selective in what they did *not* say. Certain details which we might consider essential to understanding the human aspects of the story, are usually omitted. These leave *interpretive gaps* for readers to come to the text and bring their understanding. In the OT, for example, the original story does not tell us how Noah felt about building the ark, or what Abraham was thinking when he left Ur. The writer of Hebrews, however, writing thousands of years later under the guidance of the Holy Spirit, filled in those gaps.

> By faith Noah, when warned about things not yet seen, **in holy fear** built an ark to save his family. – Hebrews 11:7

> By faith Abraham … **was looking forward** to the city with foundations, whose architect and builder is God. – Hebrews 11:8,10

The author of Hebrews, building on the theme of faith, connects the stories of the Patriarchs to his contemporary audience and fills in two interpretive gaps as he was led by the Holy Spirit. We can assume he had pastoral purpose—and so did God. By assigning human emotions and motives to the characters in the story, he is able to make it relevant to his audience.

This is the way we should connect stories to those we pray for. We connect people to stories in the Bible by the emotions and intents of the person we are praying for. The fact that we do not know the thoughts of the characters in most Bible stories makes them *more* applicable to people, not less, because the Spirit can highlight or ascribe a variety of things to that person.

For example, Abraham likely went through all kinds of emotions on his journey: loneliness in the desert, hope for a better future, fear in Egypt, astonishment when he left with its riches, disappointment when Lot separated from him. These are all possible connection points for us when we pray and minister to someone. We can connect the experiences Abraham had to the experiences in a person's life by what Abraham may have felt or thought, as God leads us. It can happen in either order: when we pray, God may show us Abraham first and sift through our understanding of Abraham to bring us to the correct touchpoint in the person's life, or he may reveal the touchpoint first and lead us to applying Abraham as a summary of what is going on.

KEYNOTE STORIES

Every story in the Bible, including the smallest ones, have the potential to come to life when you are given an application. Understanding how to apply stories can also bring the Bible to life for you. Try to familiarize yourself with all the major stories so you can use their basic points of correspondence to contemporary situations when you minister. Let's look at a couple.

Abraham

Abraham is called to leave his family and everything he knows to follow God. This is the same thing that we as Christians are called to do. Therefore we can liken Abraham's journey to our own journey through life.

One of Abraham's personal weaknesses is how much he wants a family. God spends 30 years trying to separate him from his family. First his father, Terah, then his nephew, Lot, then his illegitimate son, Ishmael, before he can have Isaac. Finally God has Abraham put Isaac on the altar, surrendering his lifelong dream to Him. When we are pursuing our God-dream, we face moments of decision where we must surrender our own goals and agenda to God's.

Moses

Moses had an amazing calling on his life. His family put themselves at great risk for him to fulfill that calling. He was raised as a child of extreme privilege in the royal family—the would-be prince of the world. He then came to a place of decision and decided to leave his lavish lifestyle in order to fulfill his calling. Most of us have a similar experience of "leaving Egypt" in order to follow God.

After leaving Egypt, Moses finds himself in the wilderness and displays great courage in defending some helpless women. God uses this to open a door of provision for him in the desert. He spends the remaining years of his strength there and then at 80 years old, likely after he has already given up, has a dramatic encounter with God. Many of us go through seasons of desperation, where we have lost hope, but God can use you mightily even in your later years.

After rising to leadership, Moses has to muster great courage and faith to obey God and confront Pharaoh. Once Pharaoh is defeated, Moses then leads Israel into the desert where they complain continuously and reject both Moses and God. Moses succeeds at everything, but in the end his temper costs him the chance to enter the Promised Land. We can see identify in this phase of his life the challenges of leadership, especially spiritual leadership.

David

David was a nobody. He was so rejected that when the most important person in the country, God's prophet Samuel came to the house, David was not even called. David was then chosen to be the future king, although nothing happened right away. He stepped forward onto the national scene by displaying great bravery in the midst of a war showdown and national crisis. He became favored by the existing king, Saul, but Saul hated him for his success. There are many touchpoints here, including being overlooked, having your destiny on delay, and seizing opportunity when all seems hopeless.

This led David to a very dark period where Saul tried to kill him, David fell in with desperate men, and even went over to the camp of the enemy for a time. Eventually Saul was killed and David rose to power. After achieving power, David became corrupted by the trappings of power and had a man killed to cover his affair with a woman. This led to a horrible family feud which left some of his children dead and consumed the rest of his life. Yet, God showed him amazing favor for his valor, devotion, and transparency. We can easily connect to David's struggle with sin, as well as his zealous desire to follow God while being persecuted by existing authorities.

Jesus and the Disciples

We often identify with the disciples, especially Peter, but since Jesus was God, sometimes we fail to connect our story to His. We must recognize that His life was the life of a perfect *man*. He sought the Father from a young age and was obedient to His parents. When He came of age, He submitted to the ministry of John the Baptist before going through an intense period of testing, where He was offered pleasure and success. When He turned these down, He returned with authority over Satan to drive out demons, heal, and do the miraculous. He started His own ministry and trained His followers to do likewise. His obedience to the Father led to increasing conflict with religious authorities. He obeyed all the way through loss of family, possessions, reputation, friends, to the point of death.

Jesus' life and ministry are a pattern which provide the perfect model for our lives. We connect to His life not as a type, but as the perfect model of behavior. It's not, "You're like Jesus in this way," but rather, "Be like Jesus in this way." We also can identify with some of His life experiences, including loneliness, drivenness, and persecution. Jesus desires to connect with us through touchpoints like these.

Other Important Characters

There are dozens of important characters in the Bible, and hundreds of less important ones, but below are a few of the main characters in the Bible we should be familiar with if we want to use Biblical stories when we pray.

- The stories of **Joseph**, **Daniel** and **Esther** furnish great material for those who are seeking advancement in hierarchical systems such as the corporate, political or church world.
- The stories of **Nehemiah** and **Ezra** are great material for those who are seeking to launch new things or fix complicated problems.
- The stories of **Ruth**, **Naomi,** and **Hannah** provide many great examples of women facing the particular challenges of womanhood – abandonment, desire for children, loneliness, the need for security.
- **Samuel**, **Elijah** and **Elisha** each are models of a prophetic lifestyle and of the spiritual warfare we all face.
- **Gideon**, **Samson** and **Joshua** all provide models of courage in the face of adversity.
- **Solomon** and his writings are the model of wise leadership.

QUESTIONS

1. Can you see the characters in the Bible as real men? Would anything change if you realized they had real emotions, choices, problems that made them free, unsure, wounded...like us?
2. Have you ever received counsel or prayer that likened you to a particular person or story in the Bible? What was your take away from that?

ACTIVATION

Pray the Story: Divide into two or three smaller groups and put someone in the middle. Ask God to reveal a Bible story or moment in a Bible story which connects to the life of that person. Look for the connection point in the story between that person and the person you are praying for. Then "pray the story" over the person's life, for example: "You are like Jacob. You are wrestling with God... but as you surrender to Him, He'll do amazing things."

STEPS YOU CAN TAKE

1. Start a study of Bible stories in a new way, with prophetic eyes. Allow God to bring out the human emotions and experiences of a particular character, to bring him/her to life. Write down any possible touchpoints you see for contemporary situations, which God can use as you minister to others.
2. Start a topical list of attributes, and arrange Bible characters you know under them—faith, perseverance, godliness, boldness... If you have time, re-read some of those stories and situations so God can bring them to mind as you minister.